© Stonewell Healing Press, 2025
All rights reserved.

This book is a labor of care. Please do not copy, share, or distribute any part of it—digitally or physically—without written permission from the author or publisher, except for brief excerpts used in reviews or critical articles. Your respect helps this work reach others who need it.

This workbook is not a replacement for therapy, crisis support, or mental health treatment. It's meant to offer reflection, comfort, and growth—not clinical care. If you're struggling, please reach out to a licensed professional. You matter too much to go through it alone.

Every effort has been made to ensure this content is accurate, responsible, and thoughtful. The author and publisher cannot guarantee outcomes and are not liable for misuse or misinterpretation of the material.

Thank you for being here. We're honored to walk beside you.

M. Tourangeau
Stonewell Healing Press

TABLE OF CONTENTS

SECTION 1 - 12
The Impact of Foster Care

SECTION 2- 40
Love with Strings Attached

SECTION 3 - 58
The Story I Was Told vs. the One I Lived

SECTION 4 - 86
Grieving the Family That Wasn't (or Wasn't Safe)

SECTION 5- 112
Who Am I Without a Mirror?

SECTION 6 136
The Good, the Bad, and the Scars

SECTION 7 164
Facing What the System Took

Stonewell Healing Press

TABLE OF CONTENTS

SECTION 8 -   **194**
The Inner Child I Still Carry

SECTION 9-   **216**
Rebuilding Safety

SECTION 10 -   **236**
Anger, Grief, and the System That Let Me Down

SECTION 11 -   **256**
Love, Connection, and the People Who Tried

SECTION 12 -   **276**
Parenting Myself Now – Healing the Abandonment Wound

SECTION 13 -   **302**
Living with the Longing – What If I Never Get the Family I Deserved?

SECTION 14 -   **322**
A Life That's Fully Mine – Reclaiming Power, Choice, and Voice

Stonewell Healing Press

Dedicated to the kids who packed
their childhoods into black trash bags.

STONEWELL HEALING PRESS

HOW TO USE THIS WORKBOOK

Take your time with this. The more you pause to really think about each question and answer honestly, the more space you create for reflection. And with deeper reflection, this experience can open up new understanding and healing you might not expect.

Be honest with yourself—there's no judgment here. This is your private space. If you want, you can even throw this book away or burn it later to keep your secrets safe. That said, be mindful of how much you dive in. Healing and reflection around tough, sensitive topics can bring up strong feelings—and yes, it can get triggering. So here's your gentle trigger warning.

The real progress comes when you practice the skills, not just read about them. The more you try them out in your life, the more helpful this workbook will be.

STONEWELL HEALING PRESS

ASSESSMENT

WHERE AM I NOW?

Before we begin, take a moment to honestly check in with yourself by rating these statements on a scale from 1 (not at all) to 10 (completely):

1-10

1. I feel like I belong in my own life — like I have a home inside myself.

2. I can face the pain of my foster care experiences without shrinking, hiding, or running away.

3. I can comfort and stand with the child I once was, even when they feel scared or abandoned.

4. II can make choices for myself without fear, guilt, or feeling undeserving.

5. I can experience love, connection, and trust without bracing for loss or betrayal.

6. I can speak my truth — even if my voice shakes, even if it feels risky.

7. I can hold the messy, complicated story of my past without feeling broken or "less than."

8. I feel I have the power to create a life that is truly mine — full of choice, meaning, and hope.

SECTION ONE

The Impact of Foster Care

There's a grief that lives in the body long before we have words for it — the grief of growing up in a world where "home" never meant safety. If you lived in foster care, you may have learned to scan every room for danger. You may have learned to freeze instead of ask for help, to make yourself small, to stay ready for goodbye. And maybe, even now, years later, your nervous system still lives as if something might be taken from you at any moment.

This section isn't about blaming your body, your brain, or your reactions. It's about understanding that everything you did — every numb feeling, every panic attack, every moment you pushed love away — was a form of protection. You adapted to survive. And now, if you're ready, we'll begin gently reconnecting with the parts of you that never got to feel truly safe. Not because you failed — but because the system did.

Making Sense Of It
The Child Who Still Waits for Home

Growing up in foster care leaves an imprint that is not always visible but is deeply felt. When you are moved between homes, told to pack your life into a garbage bag, or reminded in small ways that you are "temporary," the message that seeps into your body is that nothing is secure. Home isn't safe; love isn't steady; belonging is negotiable. Even if you found a family that treated you with kindness, the instability before or after shapes how your nervous system organizes itself. Safety becomes conditional.

Children learn about the world not through lectures, but through repetition. If the people who were supposed to stay didn't, your body learned to prepare for loss. If caregivers yelled, hit, withheld, or ignored you, your body learned that love is something to endure rather than trust. This isn't a moral failing. It's adaptation. A child cannot rewrite the rules of the house they live in. What they can do is survive. And survival often means learning to silence needs, predict moods, or leave before being left.

When children grow up inside systems designed for efficiency rather than intimacy, they learn to armor themselves. This armor often lingers well into adulthood. Maybe you notice it when someone gets close and you feel like pushing them away before they have the chance to hurt you. Maybe it shows up as a tight chest when someone says, "I love you," or a suspicion that any kindness must come with strings attached. These are not random quirks of your personality — they are the body's record of everything it had to live through.

Making Sense Of It
The Child Who Still Waits for Home

One of the cruelest legacies of foster care is that it teaches children to doubt their own worth. If you were moved from placement to placement, it can feel like you were "too much" or "not enough" for people to keep. But the truth is the system was built on scarcity and bureaucracy, not your unworthiness. Case workers were overburdened. Families were underprepared. The problem was structural — not personal. Yet the shame falls on the child, because children assume everything is about them. That shame grows up with you, until you begin to name it for what it really is: misplaced responsibility.

Healing begins when you start to separate what was yours from what was never yours to carry. The grief of foster care is not just about what happened, but also about what didn't happen — the steady hugs, the safe dinners, the rituals of family life that many people take for granted. That absence is real. It deserves mourning. And it deserves compassion, because grieving what you never had is just as legitimate as grieving what you lost.

The impact of foster care is layered: nervous systems wired for vigilance, attachment styles shaped by inconsistency, identities marked by "otherness." And yet, you are not only what happened to you. The same strategies that once kept you alive — scanning, protecting, enduring — can be re-shaped into strengths. Hyper-vigilance becomes intuition. Independence becomes resilience. Knowing how to read a room becomes emotional intelligence.

What did "safety" mean to me growing up?

Safety isn't just physical — it's emotional, too. Take time to reflect: when you were a child, what made you feel safest? What made you feel unsafe? Who or what did you turn to when things were hard? This is not to judge your past — but to witness how your body learned what safety looked like.

What did "safety" mean to me growing up?

How did my body learn to survive?

Did you freeze? Fawn? Dissociate? Rage? Consider what your survival strategies were as a child. Were you quiet and compliant, always trying to be "good"? Or maybe loud and reactive to keep people at a distance? Gently explore how those behaviors protected you.

How did my body learn to survive?

What happens in my body when I feel threatened, even now?

Pay attention to sensations — tight chest, fast heartbeat, numbness, stomach pain, disconnection. When something feels emotionally unsafe, what does your body do? When did you first learn that response?

What happens in my body when I feel threatened, even now?

When have I mistaken survival for strength?

Sometimes we're praised for being "resilient," when what we really were was unsupported. Were there times you seemed strong or independent, but inside you felt alone, scared, or numb? Let yourself rewrite that story with compassion.

When have I mistaken survival for strength?

Where do I still carry fear, even if my life is "safe" now?

Safety isn't just about your environment — it's about what your body believes. Explore any ways your nervous system still acts like danger is nearby, even if things seem stable now. There is no shame in this. It's information.

Where do I still carry fear, even if my life is "safe" now?

What would safety actually feel like in my body today?

Let yourself imagine: what does it feel like to be safe — not just in theory, but in your bones? Maybe it's warmth in your chest, deep breaths, or soft eyes. Describe it fully, even if you've never felt it before. You deserve to.

What would safety actually feel like in my body today?

TRACING THE TRUTH

THE ARMOR YOU WORE

In foster care, survival often meant building armor — ways of hiding, shutting down, or toughening up so you could make it through. That armor wasn't weakness. It was brilliance. It kept you alive in an environment where safety wasn't guaranteed. Now, as an adult, you get to examine that armor with compassion. Instead of ripping it off, we'll honor it.

Why it helps:
By naming and honoring your armor, you shift from self-blame to self-recognition. Instead of seeing old survival patterns as flaws, you recognize them as protective strategies. This begins to regulate the nervous system, because gratitude softens shame. You don't have to drop your armor overnight — you just have to stop hating it. When you see it with kindness, your body feels safer loosening its grip.

Write down 3–5 ways you learned to protect yourself in foster care (ex: staying quiet, never asking for help, being "the funny one").
Next to each, write what it protected you from.
Place your hand on your heart and say: "Thank you for keeping me safe."

TRACING THE TRUTH

THE ARMOR YOU WORE

TRACING THE TRUTH

THE HEAVIEST BAGS

Many who grew up in foster care remember the weight of a bag — sometimes a trash bag, sometimes a suitcase, sometimes nothing at all. That bag became a symbol of instability: your life reduced to what you could carry in your hands. This exercise uses the image of the bag to honor what you've carried — and to begin unpacking what no longer belongs to you.

Why it helps:
The bag exercise turns an old wound into a visual metaphor you can work with. Instead of your survival being invisible, you give it shape and acknowledgment. By writing what you carried, you validate the enormity of what was placed on your shoulders as a child. By naming what was missing, you remind yourself that the gap was never your fault. And by choosing one thing to unpack, you create a small act of reclamation — teaching your body that you no longer have to keep carrying the same old weight.

Inside the bag, write down the things you carried in foster care: burdens, fears, responsibilities, secrets.
Around the bag, write the things you should have been given instead: stability, safety, unconditional love.
Choose one item inside the bag you are ready to "unpack." Write it out honestly.

TRACING THE TRUTH

THE HEAVIEST BAGS

TRACING THE TRUTH

THE HEAVIEST BAGS

TRACING THE TRUTH

A LETTER TO THE CHILD YOU WERE

Children in foster care often grow up without steady reassurance. No one consistently said, "You matter. You are safe. You are loved." This exercise is a way to give that back to yourself. Writing to your younger self helps bridge the gap between what you needed then and what you can offer now.

Why it helps:
Your nervous system holds onto the unmet needs of your younger self. By writing to them, you give those needs acknowledgment. This practice doesn't erase what happened, but it rewrites the message your body carries: that you were never unworthy, only unsupported. It strengthens self-compassion and builds a bridge between past and present, teaching your body that care can come from within.

Imagine yourself at a specific age in foster care. Picture their face, their posture, their worry.
Write a letter beginning with, "Dear [your name], I see you..."
Include words of comfort you wish someone had told you.

TRACING THE TRUTH

A LETTER TO THE CHILD YOU WERE

TRACING THE TRUTH

A LETTER TO THE CHILD YOU WERE

TRACING THE TRUTH

A LETTER TO THE CHILD YOU WERE

TRACING THE TRUTH

A LETTER TO THE CHILD YOU WERE

Every way you learned to cope was a form of wisdom, shaped by systems that never should have failed you. You get to keep what helped and let go of what hurts — at your pace, on your terms. Safety is no longer something you have to chase or earn. It's something we will slowly, build — from the inside out.

SECTION TWO

Love with Strings Attached

If you've ever pushed someone away even though you needed them, or clung tightly to someone even when it hurt, you're not broken — you're just wired for protection. Love, for many of us who lived through foster care, never came clean. It came with conditions. With paperwork. With time limits. With fear.

You may have learned that love meant performing. Or disappearing. Or pretending to be fine. Maybe the adults who were supposed to love you were the ones who hurt you. Maybe the ones who stayed were always one conversation away from leaving. No wonder love doesn't feel simple.

This section isn't about fixing how you attach — it's about understanding why your heart learned to guard itself. There's nothing wrong with needing love, and nothing weak about fearing it. Let's gently untangle the rules you learned about love… and rewrite them, piece by piece, in your own language.

Making Sense Of It
What Happens When Love Comes With Conditions

If love arrived with forms to fill, deadlines, and small-print clauses, your heart would learn to read legalese before it learned to breathe. That's the quiet cruelty of growing up inside systems or homes where affection was conditional: you learned to negotiate safety the way other kids learned to tie shoelaces. Perform well, don't ask too much, be grateful for crumbs — and maybe, just maybe, someone will stay. Those rules didn't come from you. They were taught to keep you safer in unstable places. But they also rewired how you seek, receive, and trust closeness.

When adults give love with strings — affection that's earned, withheld, transactional, or time-limited — the child inside you translates that into survival logic. You learn that love is a currency and you become a skilled economist of affection: you budget how much need you can spend, you invest in pleasing, you hedge against abandonment. That economy creates attachment styles people try to fix later: clinging as a hedge against loss, pushing away to avoid being disappointed, or moving between both in a dizzying loop when signals are mixed. These aren't personality flaws. They are strategies that helped a younger you stay alive.

You might recognize the choreography: you soften and perform when approval is on the table; you go silent when criticism is near. You may replay the same scripts in adult relationships — becoming the "always available" partner who forgets their own needs, or the "impenetrable" person who keeps everyone at arm's length to avoid being hurt. Or both.

Making Sense Of It
What Happens When Love Comes With Conditions

Underneath every strategy sits a basic calculation: predictability reduces pain. If love can't be predicted, your nervous system will try to make it calculable — through rules, monitoring, code-switching, people-pleasing, or leaving first.

The emotional currency of conditional love teaches a child to distrust their own feelings. If your joy made caregivers uncomfortable, or your grief didn't get mirrored, you learned to archive emotional experience rather than to share it. Over time, this creates a private ledger of needs that feels risky to open. "If I ask," the ledger whispers, "I will be denied." So you start to ration vulnerability, to ration requests for help, to ration hope.

There's also the hidden shame: the sense that if you're not meeting the unspoken contract, you are the problem. That one is corrosive because it turns systemic failure into personal defect. It's crucial to separate the architecture from the human. Paperwork, case numbers, staff turnover, under-resourced homes — these are systems that fail children. Shame that lives on your shoulders is misplaced, though it's understandable you carry it. Recognizing that is an act of reparenting: it loosens the belief that love is something to be earned rather than a human right.

Making Sense Of It
What Happens When Love Comes With Conditions

Healing from love-with-strings isn't about erasing your caution or pretending your defenses don't make sense. It's about teaching your heart to tolerate a different grammar of care. How? By learning to notice the rules you were taught, naming them, and then deciding — with curiosity, not judgment — whether those rules serve you now. Maybe some do; hyper-awareness can be protective in certain contexts. But when a rule prevents you from resting in the presence of genuine safety, it's time to edit it.

This work is also practical: it means practicing small taste-tests of connection that don't demand radical change overnight. Let someone show up without an agenda. Ask for what you need in a low-stakes moment. Give yourself permission to receive a kindness without "paying it back" immediately. Each successful instance rewrites a little line in the ledger: not all care requires a receipt.

Most of all, remember this: the rules you learned about love were not moral failures — they were survival instructions. The person they shaped is resourceful, adaptive, and durable. The truer work now is learning how to let your heart down, slowly, in places that look and feel different. That doesn't make you soft or reckless. It makes you human — and that humanity deserves care without strings.

What did I learn I had to do to be loved?

Were you praised for being "easy"? Quiet? Perfect? Reflect on the rules you absorbed about love — even the unspoken ones. Did you have to earn love? Did you believe love could vanish if you weren't good enough?

What did I learn I had to do to be loved?

When has love felt unsafe, unpredictable, or painful?

Think about moments where love and harm were tangled. Were there people who said they cared for you... but still hurt you? Or people who cared for you, but weren't safe to rely on? Let yourself name the contradictions.

When has love felt unsafe, unpredictable, or painful?

What does "closeness" bring up in me — hope, fear, both?

Notice your body's reaction to emotional closeness. Do you pull away, or cling tighter? Do you feel calm, or on edge? There's no wrong answer. Just curiosity.

What does "closeness" bring up in me — hope, fear, both?

When have I sabotaged connection to protect myself?

Think of times you ghosted someone, started a fight, shut down, or backed away when things got too good. What were you trying to protect? What did that part of you need?

When have I sabotaged connection to protect myself?

What kind of love do I long for — and do I believe it exists for me?

Dare to name what you wish for in love. Not what you think you deserve, but what your heart truly craves. Safe. Consistent. Real. Can you imagine someone loving you without needing you to earn it?

What kind of love do I long for — and do I believe it exists for me?

TRACING THE TRUTH

THE TABLE OF TERMS

If love felt like a contract, it had terms — often unspoken. This exercise invites you to rewrite the terms of how you want to be loved now. Think of it as co-authoring a new agreement with yourself (and future partners) — one that names boundaries, needs, and the simple rights you wish you'd been given.

Why it helps:
Creating a Table of Terms gives language to what often feels like vague longing. Naming expectations reduces cognitive load and creates clear experiments for real-world interaction. This turns hope into observable data: either the environment responds in the way you need, or you learn to adjust your boundaries. Both outcomes are useful. The table trains your nervous system to expect clarity and reduces the toxic waiting that conditional love taught you. It's a map for choosing where to invest trust.

Fill 3–5 terms you want in future relationships (ex: "I have the right to rest," "I can ask for help without retaliation").
For each term, write a small, practical way to test it in the next month (a conversation, a boundary, a request).

TRACING THE TRUTH

THE TABLE OF TERMS

Term	Why It Matters	How You'll Test It

SECTION THREE

The Story I Was Told vs. the One I Lived

There's a story people love to tell about foster kids — that we're "resilient," "so strong," "so lucky someone took us in." That we should be grateful. That we should smile and not cause too much trouble. That we should be thankful just to have survived. But here's the truth: gratitude doesn't cancel grief. Strength doesn't mean silence. And just because someone fed you and gave you a bed doesn't mean you felt safe, seen, or loved.

Maybe you were the "easy" one. Or the angry one. Or the one who made yourself disappear. Maybe you learned to act okay so no one would dig too deep. And maybe that story became a cage.

In this section, we're going to gently crack open the version of your story the world wanted you to tell — and make space for the one that actually happened. Your truth deserves to exist, even if it's messy. Especially if it's messy.

Making Sense Of It
The Cage of Other People's Stories

When you grow up in foster care, you don't just experience a series of placements — you inherit a narrative that others write for you. Society, teachers, caseworkers, even well-meaning family members often reduce the foster care experience to a set of digestible labels: resilient, strong, lucky, grateful. On paper, these words sound like praise. In reality, they can feel like a cage. They flatten nuance, silence anger, and erase the messy, complicated truth of what you lived.

The child inside you learns early that some feelings are acceptable, while others must be hidden. You are allowed gratitude, but anger or fear is messy and risky. You are praised for survival, but mourning the absence of safety is unwelcome. The system — and sometimes the people within it — reward compliance. You learn to nod, to smile, to be the "easy" child, the quiet achiever, the adaptable one. That version of yourself gets applause. The version that cries, rages, or resists often has to hide. Over time, this creates an internalized editor: a voice that polices your story, censoring the parts that might make someone uncomfortable.

This censoring is survival. It was a way to protect yourself from judgment, punishment, or further rejection. But as an adult, the effect is that your own experience becomes filtered, muted, or even denied. You might find yourself telling the world the story it wants to hear — "I'm fine," "I'm grateful," "I survived" — while your private narrative carries grief, confusion, and lingering fear. Both stories exist simultaneously, creating tension, self-doubt, and sometimes shame.

Making Sense Of It
The Cage of Other People's Stories

One of the most insidious effects of this imposed narrative is that it can make you doubt your own memory. You may question: Was it really that bad? Am I exaggerating? Should I be grateful for what I had? That doubt is understandable. When survival depends on compliance and appeasement, your mind prioritizes others' perceptions over your internal truth. You become skilled at fitting into someone else's story, often at the expense of your own.

Healing begins when you start to separate the story you were told you had to live from the story you actually lived. That means naming all the versions of yourself: the compliant child, the disappearing child, the angry child, the sad child — and holding space for each. Every feeling you had was valid, and every reaction was an adaptation. Your truth is not wrong or ungrateful; it is real.

Reclaiming your story is also about noticing what has been left out. Maybe the world celebrated your achievements but never witnessed your tears. Maybe you were admired for resilience but never asked whether you felt safe. The gaps between what was acknowledged and what was experienced are where grief hides, where shame lingers, and where healing begins. By intentionally telling the story you actually lived, you teach your nervous system that it is safe to feel your feelings, to mourn what was lost, and to take up the space that was denied to you.

What was the story I was expected to tell about my life?

Think about how others framed your experience — foster parents, caseworkers, teachers, even strangers. Were you praised for being strong? Encouraged to "move on"? What parts of your truth were left out or silenced?

What was the story I was expected to tell about my life?

What parts of my real story didn't fit that version?

Were there things you couldn't say? Anger you weren't allowed to feel? Pain no one acknowledged? Write freely here — no filters, no performance. Just truth.

What parts of my real story didn't fit that version?

What did I learn about expressing anger, grief, or disappointment?

Was it safe to say "this isn't okay"? Were you punished, ignored, or shamed for being upset? How did you learn to stuff things down in order to be accepted?

The Story I Was Told vs. the One I Lived

What did I learn about expressing anger, grief, or disappointment?

When have I felt ashamed for feeling what I feel?

Even now, do you judge yourself for being sad, angry, or distant? Do you feel guilty for not feeling grateful enough? Explore where that shame lives in your body and your story.

The Story I Was Told vs. the One I Lived

When have I felt ashamed for feeling what I feel?

What's one thing I wish someone had said to me when I was struggling?

Imagine someone kind — someone who sees the whole you — sitting across from you now. What would they say? What would you want to hear?

What's one thing I wish someone had said to me when I was struggling?

What would it feel like to tell the whole truth, and still be loved?

Let yourself imagine it. You don't have to share it with anyone else. But what if you could speak your story — with all its cracks — and still be worthy of love? That's what we're building here.

_____

_____

_____

_____

_____

_____

_____

_____

_____

_____

_____

_____

_____

The Story I Was Told vs. the One I Lived

What would it feel like to tell the whole truth, and still be loved?

TRACING THE TRUTH

THE SHADOW SKETCH

Parts of your story have likely been hidden, like shadows that never fully disappear. Drawing your "shadow self" helps you bring those pieces into awareness — not to judge them, but to recognize their presence and the resilience they represent.

Why it helps:
Visualizing shadowed parts externalizes feelings that may have been denied or minimized. The act of drawing and acknowledging them reinforces nervous system safety: these parts are seen, not dangerous, and you can hold them with compassion. Over time, this builds integration, allowing previously suppressed experiences to coexist with the parts of you that were praised or visible. The shadow becomes not a mark of shame but evidence of survival, strength, and complexity.

On paper, outline a figure representing yourself.
Fill in the figure with words, images, or colors representing the parts of your story you've kept hidden.
Around the figure, write words of recognition or gratitude for each shadowed part.

TRACING THE TRUTH

THE SHADOW SKETCH

TRACING THE TRUTH

THE TABLE OF TRUTHS

Sometimes the version of your story the world applauded is not the one you want to live by anymore. This exercise creates a "table" where all parts of your experience can sit without judgment — the parts that were messy, confusing, or painful. By giving each feeling or experience a seat, you witness it, honor it, and begin to reclaim authorship of your story.

Why it helps:
This exercise externalizes and validates the multiplicity of your experience. By giving each part a seat at the table, you send a message to your nervous system: it is safe to feel, to remember, and to honor all of you. Over time, acknowledging these truths diminishes internalized judgment and shame, allowing you to carry a fuller, richer story — one that includes grief, resilience, anger, and joy without forcing any single part to dominate or disappear.

Draw a table on paper with enough seats for all parts of your younger self.
Label each seat with a version of yourself: "angry child," "quiet achiever," "grateful survivor," etc.
Write one truth that each version wants acknowledged in the corresponding seat.
Spend a few minutes silently reading all the truths aloud to yourself.

TRACING THE TRUTH

THE TABLE OF TRUTHS

TRACING THE TRUTH

MY TRUE STORY

For years, the world may have asked you to tell only part of your story — the parts that were palatable, neat, or "inspiring." But your life is not a highlight reel. Your truth is messy, complicated, and layered — and it deserves to exist exactly as it happened. This exercise gives you a safe, contained space to write your story fully, without editing for what others will think. There's no wrong way to do this: no timeline, no filter, no expectation. This is for you, for your younger self, and for the part of you that wants to be fully seen.

Why it helps:
Visualizing shadowed parts externalizes feelings that may have been denied or minimized. The act of drawing and acknowledging them reinforces nervous system safety: these parts are seen, not dangerous, and you can hold them with compassion. Over time, this builds integration, allowing previously suppressed experiences to coexist with the parts of you that were praised or visible. The shadow becomes not a mark of shame but evidence of survival, strength, and complexity.

Set aside a quiet space where you won't be interrupted.
Begin writing your story from the earliest memory you want to include. Include placements, foster homes, teachers, caregivers, relationships, and all emotions that arose: fear, grief, joy, anger, relief — everything.
Allow your story to flow without stopping to edit or judge. If you need breaks, pause and return, but let each memory have its moment on the page.
When you finish (or after a set time, e.g., 30–60 minutes), read it aloud to yourself if you feel safe. Optionally, save it somewhere private, or keep it in a journal to revisit.

TRACING THE TRUTH

MY TRUE STORY

TRACING THE TRUTH

MY TRUE STORY

TRACING THE TRUTH

MY TRUE STORY

TRACING THE TRUTH

MY TRUE STORY

TRACING THE TRUTH

MY TRUE STORY

You were never just a "grateful foster kid." You were a whole person, with a whole story — one that includes hurt, hope, anger, strength, numbness, survival, and love. You don't owe anyone an apology or a clean version.

SECTION FOUR

Grieving the Family That Wasn't (or Wasn't Safe)

When grief first takes over, the future feels like a door that slammed shut. All the images you held — baby showers, tiny clothes, names you whispered in secret — disappear in an instant. It can feel unbearable to imagine "what's next" when what you wanted most has been taken. But grief doesn't mean your life has ended. It means your path is changing, painfully and irrevocably — but not permanently without hope.

This section isn't about tying everything up neatly. It's about honoring the ambiguity, sitting with the unknown, and still allowing a flicker of possibility to remain lit. Whether or not you want to try again, whether or not you feel strong, you are allowed to hope again — not because you've "moved on," but because you're still here.

You get to redefine what the future means for you. You get to heal on your timeline, and carry love with you into whatever comes next.

Making Sense Of It
The Unseen Funeral

Some griefs are obvious: friends attend, cards arrive, dinners are made. Foster care grief is rarely that visible. It often sits under your skin, quietly shaping your posture, your breath, your expectations of others. You grieve people who are alive, yet emotionally absent. You grieve homes that promised security but offered instability. You grieve protection that should have existed, and sometimes, you even grieve the possibility of the family you never got to have. And yet, you may feel you don't have permission to mourn any of it.

This grief is complex because it is layered and contradictory. You may love the people who hurt you — your birth parents, siblings, or caregivers — while simultaneously recognizing they caused pain. You may long for stability while knowing it was never consistent. Many foster care survivors carry what I call "forbidden mourning": wanting something that either wasn't safe or wasn't given. Society struggles to acknowledge this type of grief because it doesn't fit into tidy narratives of loss. And so, you may have spent years suppressing your grief to protect yourself, to maintain appearances, or because someone told you to be "grateful" or "strong."

Suppression is a form of survival. It allows a child to navigate chaos with less disruption. But the body never forgets. Anger, sadness, longing, and confusion become lodged in muscle memory, nervous system tension, or emotional flashpoints. It's why, even decades later, a smell, a phrase, or a picture can bring a visceral ache. The grief was never invalid — it simply didn't have space to exist in a world that demanded resilience over mourning.

Making Sense Of It
The Unseen Funeral

Another layer is moral confusion. If your family hurt you, or if your foster placements were abusive, you may feel shame for longing for them. You might ask, "How can I miss someone who wasn't safe?" This tension is natural. Love and grief are not logical. They don't obey rules of safety or justice. Feeling loss for people who caused pain doesn't make you weak or delusional — it makes you human. The nervous system learns patterns of attachment early, and attachment often outlasts abuse.

Grieving the family that wasn't is also about reclaiming the losses that never got recognition. You might imagine a funeral that never happened, a goodbye you never had, or a celebration of the love you wished existed. This imaginative act is not fantasy — it's a neurobiological tool. The nervous system responds to symbolic rituals as if they were real, giving the brain and body a chance to process what words and events never allowed. Grief, when witnessed even symbolically, begins to move instead of stagnating.

It is important to recognize that mourning this kind of loss is not about erasing resilience or gratitude. You can grieve the absence of love while still acknowledging survival, strength, and the people who did show care. Grief and gratitude can coexist. In fact, allowing grief to be seen and held often strengthens the capacity for future connection. It teaches the nervous system that loss can be witnessed safely, and that your emotions — even complicated ones — are valid.

Who have I lost that I never got to grieve?

This could be a biological parent, a sibling, a foster parent, or even the idea of a "normal" childhood. Let yourself name the losses — even the complicated ones.

Who have I lost that I never got to grieve?

What do I miss, even if it wasn't healthy or safe?

It's okay to miss someone who hurt you. To miss a routine, a voice, or even just the idea of family. That doesn't make you weak — it makes you human.

What do I miss, even if it wasn't healthy or safe?

What am I still angry I didn't get?

Was it safety? Protection? Belonging? Someone who showed up consistently? Anger is part of grief. Let it speak.

What am I still angry I didn't get?

What would a proper goodbye look like, if it were up to me?

Imagine designing your own ceremony. Would you write a letter? Burn a photo? Sit in silence? What kind of goodbye would help you begin letting go?

What would a proper goodbye look like, if it were up to me?

What part of me is still holding on — and what does it need?

Is there a younger version of you still waiting to be chosen, or heard? What would you want to say to them now?

What part of me is still holding on — and what does it need?

How can I grieve in a way that feels sacred to me?

This doesn't have to look like anyone else's process. What feels right: tears? Art? Silence? Movement? Music? Give yourself the freedom to choose your own ritual.

How can I grieve in a way that feels sacred to me?

TRACING THE TRUTH

THE CEREMONY THAT NEVER HAPPENED

Many of us left foster care without closure. No funeral for the home we lost, no goodbye to a caregiver we loved or feared, no acknowledgment of what was absent. This exercise gives you permission to create your own symbolic ceremony — a ritual for the grief that never got witnessed.

Why it helps:
Ceremonies activate the nervous system's ability to process loss. Even symbolic rituals allow grief to move, creating a sense of witnessed closure where none existed. By naming what was lost and honoring it intentionally, you reclaim agency over your mourning. The body remembers grief, and ritual gives it a safe path to integrate. Over time, these small acts reduce the weight of unacknowledged sorrow and invite compassion for your complex feelings toward people and places that shaped you.

Gather an object or image that represents the family or home you are grieving.
Find a quiet space and create a small ritual: light a candle, play music, or sit silently.
Speak aloud or write the words you wish you could have said: "I see you. I mourn this loss. It mattered."
Optionally, place the object somewhere special or release it in a symbolic way (bury, burn safely, or tuck away).

TRACING THE TRUTH

MAPPING THE UNSEEN GRIEF

Grief from foster care is often invisible. Mapping it visually can give shape to what has been lived quietly under the skin. This exercise helps you identify the relationships, homes, and experiences you lost or never fully received, so they can be held and acknowledged.

Why it helps:
Visual mapping externalizes invisible grief and allows the nervous system to witness and contain loss. By seeing your relationships and homes laid out, you can honor what was absent or harmful while recognizing the survival it took to endure. The act of placing compassion alongside each node teaches your body that grief can coexist with safety, reducing internal tension and fostering emotional integration. This map becomes a tool for reflection and acknowledgment — a reminder that your grief is valid, held, and visible, even when others cannot see it.

Draw a large tree.
Label the roots with early placements or family connections.
On each branch, write people, homes, or moments you grieve — both safe and unsafe.
Notice which areas feel heavy, and place a symbol of compassion (heart, hand, or star) next to each.

TRACING THE TRUTH

MAPPING THE UNSEEN GRIEF

TRACING THE TRUTH

LETTERS TO THE FAMILY THAT WASN'T

You may have people in your life — birth parents, foster parents, siblings — whose presence or absence left deep marks. Writing a letter to them, even if you never send it, is a way to give voice to the feelings that were never safe to express. This is not about blame; it is about witnessing your own heart and grief.

Why it helps:
Writing letters externalizes grief and provides a container for emotions that were previously unsafe to feel. It engages cognitive, emotional, and somatic systems, helping your nervous system integrate long-held tension. By addressing the family or home directly, even symbolically, you validate your own experience and create permission to mourn. This practice reinforces that your grief is real, your feelings are valid, and that you can witness your own losses with compassion and clarity.

Choose one person, family, or home you wish to acknowledge.
Write a letter expressing your feelings honestly: longing, anger, sadness, or love.
Close the letter with a statement of self-compassion: *"I honor my experience and my heart."*

TRACING THE TRUTH

LETTERS TO THE FAMILY THAT WASN'T

TRACING THE TRUTH

LETTERS TO THE FAMILY THAT WASN'T

TRACING THE TRUTH

LETTERS TO THE FAMILY THAT WASN'T

TRACING THE TRUTH

LETTERS TO THE FAMILY THAT WASN'T

TRACING THE TRUTH

LETTERS TO THE FAMILY THAT WASN'T

SECTION FIVE

Who Am I Without a Mirror?

When you grow up in foster care, people often decide who you are for you. Files are written. Boxes are ticked. Homes come and go. You adapt. You survive. But somewhere along the way, your sense of self can start to feel like a collection of borrowed clothes — things that never quite fit.

Maybe you were raised by people who didn't share your culture, language, or values. Maybe you lost your last name. Maybe you weren't allowed to ask questions. Or maybe you've been shapeshifting for so long — trying to survive — that you're not even sure what you want, believe, or belong to anymore.

This section is about coming home to yourself — not by picking an identity off a shelf, but by building one that feels like yours. You are not too fragmented to be whole. You are not too lost to be found. You have a right to belong — to yourself, and to a life that reflects you.

Making Sense Of It
The Self in Fragments

Growing up in foster care often means growing up without a reliable mirror. Not the kind you look into in the bathroom, but the one that reflects back your identity, values, culture, and worth. Mirrors — the kind that reflect who you are in the eyes of someone who knows and accepts you — were often missing, cracked, or unreliable. Instead, you were left piecing together reflections from strangers, caseworkers, peers, and temporary caregivers. Each reflection was partial, biased, or conditional, and your young self learned quickly to adapt, survive, and shapeshift accordingly.

This process creates what I think of as the "fragmented self." Fragments are pieces of you borrowed, adopted, or shaped by necessity. Perhaps one piece learned to be "easy" so foster parents wouldn't get frustrated; another piece became invisible to avoid punishment; another piece performed well in school to gain approval or keep hope alive. Each fragment served a purpose, and each protected a vulnerable part of you. These fragments kept you alive. But now, as an adult, the patchwork may feel heavy, uncomfortable, or unfamiliar. You may look in the mirror and feel like no single piece truly belongs to you.

The loss of a stable identity can impact everything: your confidence, your relationships, and your sense of purpose. When you've spent years shapeshifting to fit others' expectations, the question "Who am I?" can feel dangerous or impossible. Asking it may stir panic: If I let go of the roles I've mastered, will I disappear? Will anyone recognize me? Will I even know who I am? These fears are rooted in survival strategies that once kept your body and heart safe.

Making Sense Of It
The Self in Fragments

Part of reclaiming identity is understanding that fragmentation is not failure. It is adaptive intelligence in response to inconsistent care. Your fragments are witnesses to your survival. Some fragments may be proud, strong, or resilient. Others may carry grief, shame, or anger. None are "wrong" or disposable. Healing starts when you honor each piece without judgment and begin to see how they contribute to your whole self.

Another challenge is cultural and familial dislocation. Many foster youth are placed in homes far from their roots, separated from language, heritage, and community. Fragments of identity may carry borrowed cultural norms or suppress your original self entirely. This dislocation adds layers to the sense of being "without a mirror," because the reflection you see may be someone else's image — safe, familiar, or approved — but not yours.

Building a coherent sense of self begins with curiosity, not judgment. Ask yourself: Which fragments are protecting me today? Which belong to someone else's story? Which feel like home? This exploration is delicate and ongoing. The goal is not perfection. It is not to erase fragments. It is to allow them to co-exist under the guidance of a conscious, adult self that can hold space for all parts, acknowledge what was learned, and choose what feels authentic moving forward.

Making Sense Of It
The Self in Fragments

Identity reclamation is also about embodied knowing. When you've had to survive in unpredictable systems, your body carries memory in posture, gestures, and habitual tension. Returning to your self means noticing how your body feels in response to different fragments and testing what feels aligned, safe, and grounded. Your nervous system has learned to scan for threats; it also needs to learn what safety, authenticity, and belonging feel like internally.

Ultimately, "Who am I without a mirror?" is not a question of finding a single label, but of authoring your internal narrative. It's building a sense of self that reflects your values, desires, culture, and experiences. A self that's yours — not borrowed, performed, or curated for someone else's approval. This work is gentle, patient, and ongoing, but each step toward integration strengthens self-trust, grounding, and the capacity to receive love from yourself and others.

Your fragments are not weaknesses. They are living archives of resilience, courage, and survival. Healing is not about polishing them until they all match. It is about honoring them, listening, and weaving a self that is coherent, flexible, and fully yours.

Who told me who I was — and did it ever feel true?

Think about caseworkers, foster families, schools, even your birth family. What labels or expectations were placed on you? Did they reflect who you actually are?

Who told me who I was — and did it ever feel true?

What parts of me did I have to hide to stay safe or be accepted?

This could be language, culture, gender identity, emotions, or even dreams. What did you silence or shrink — and what do those parts want now?

What parts of me did I have to hide to stay safe or be accepted?

What does "belonging" mean to me — and have I ever felt it?

Explore moments where you felt seen, welcomed, or connected. What made those moments feel real? Where do you long to feel that again?

What does "belonging" mean to me — and have I ever felt it?

What do I know — or wonder — about my culture, ancestry, or roots?

Even if you don't have the full story, what threads are calling you? What would you love to explore if it were safe to do so?

What do I know — or wonder — about my culture, ancestry, or roots?

If I could create a space or community that felt fully like home, what would it include?

Who would be there? What values, food, music, language, or rituals would exist? This isn't just imagination — it's a blueprint for healing.

If I could create a space or community that felt fully like home, what would it include?

What feels most "me" — even if I can't explain why?

Is there something you wear, listen to, say, or believe that just feels right? Trust those signals. Identity doesn't need permission to be valid.

What feels most "me" — even if I can't explain why?

Who am I becoming, now that I don't have to survive the same way?

When you stop fighting to just exist, who do you get to be? You might still be discovering it — and that's okay.

Who am I becoming, now that I don't have to survive the same way?

TRACING THE TRUTH

THE TABLE THAT WASN'T THERE

Family dinners, holiday rituals, and everyday tables often symbolize belonging. For many in foster care, the table was unstable — sometimes welcoming, sometimes unsafe, sometimes missing altogether. This exercise helps you imagine the table you always needed.

Why it helps:
By envisioning your own table, you reclaim the power to create belonging on your terms. Instead of replaying the absence of stability, you map out a vision of safety and connection that can guide your future relationships. The nervous system responds to imagery, and this exercise plants a felt sense of possibility: that the table you once longed for can be built, piece by piece, in your adult life.

Draw a table.
Place around it (in words or drawings) the people, objects, or symbols that would make you feel safe.
At the center of the table, write one value you want this table to hold (ex: honesty, kindness, consistency).
Keep the image as a reminder that you can build new tables now.

TRACING THE TRUTH

THE TABLE THAT WASN'T THERE

TRACING THE TRUTH

THE FRAGMENT MAP

Your sense of self may feel like scattered pieces of glass, each reflecting someone else's version of you. This exercise helps you map the fragments — what parts of you were shaped by survival, adaptation, or other people's expectations — so you can begin to notice, honor, and integrate them. By putting your fragments on paper, you start to see the bigger picture: the whole self that exists beneath the fractured surface.

Why it helps:
This visual exercise externalizes internal complexity and gives structure to the parts of you that feel scattered. Seeing your fragments allows your nervous system to acknowledge and hold them safely, rather than repress or ignore them. By identifying purpose and value in each piece, you move from fragmented survival toward conscious integration. This cultivates a grounded sense of self, strengthens self-trust, and lays the foundation for making choices aligned with your authentic identity.

The large circle to represent your current sense of self.
Inside the circle, add smaller shapes or circles representing distinct fragments (e.g., "the quiet child," "the achiever," "the shapeshifter," "the angry protector").
Next to each fragment, write its purpose: why it existed, what it protected, or what it accomplished.
Reflect on which fragments feel most like you today and which you want to nurture or integrate further.

TRACING THE TRUTH

THE FRAGMENT MAP

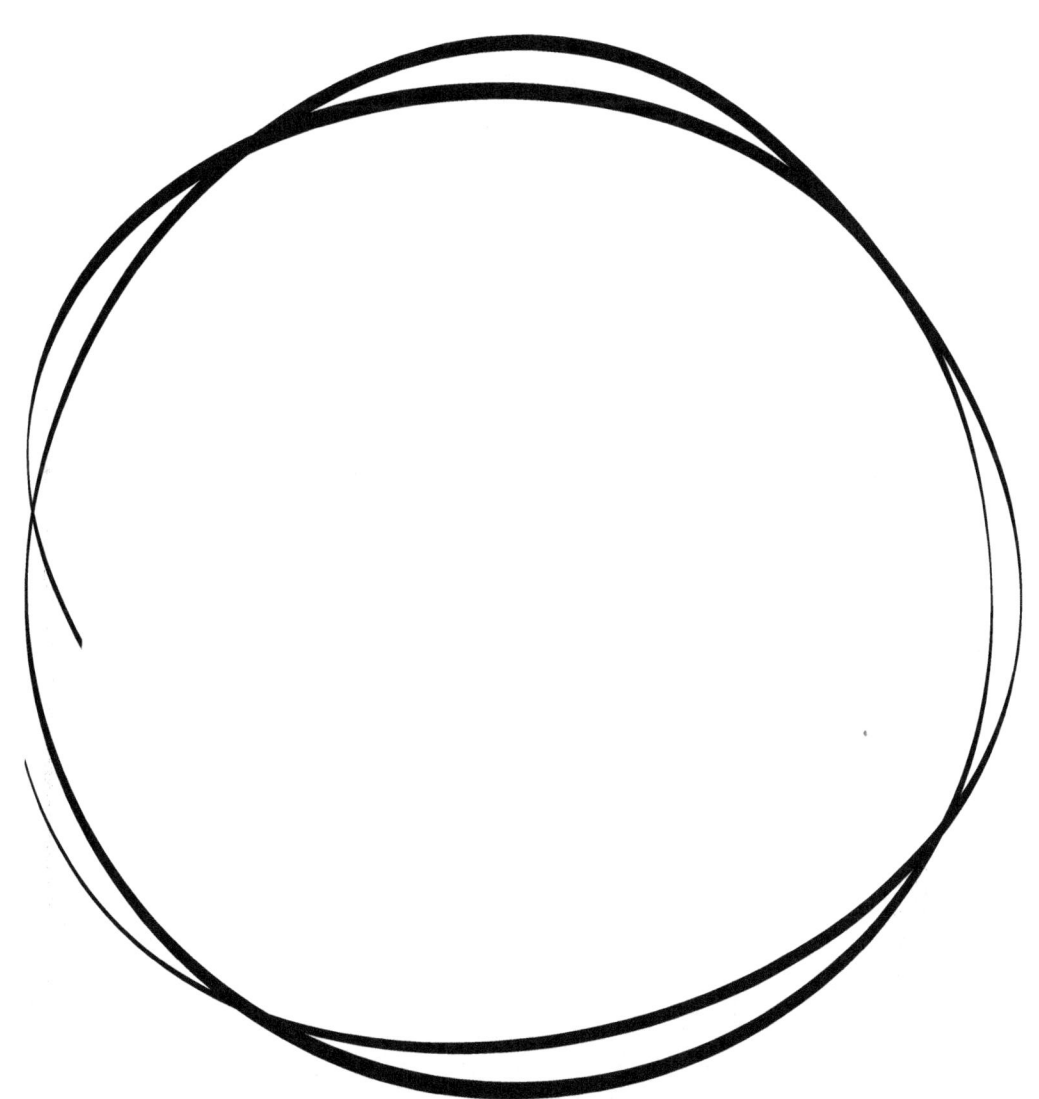

SECTION SIX

The Good, the Bad, and the Scars

It's not always black and white. Sometimes the people who hurt you also helped you. Sometimes the house was clean, the fridge was full — and yet, you felt invisible. Sometimes a foster parent made you feel safe for the first time. Sometimes they destroyed your trust. Sometimes it was all of that, in the same home, in the same year.

This chapter is here to hold all of it — the kindness, the cruelty, the disappointment, the confusion, the bonds that still ache, and the ones you're not sure how to name. Because you're allowed to love someone and still be angry. You're allowed to be grateful and still feel grief.

There's no "right" way to feel about your foster care experiences. There's only your truth — and you deserve space to tell it without needing to explain, justify, or filter. Let's make room for the whole story.

Making Sense Of It
The Patchwork Quilt of Experience

Foster care rarely gives you a tidy story. Life inside the system is full of contrasts: warmth and neglect, kindness and cruelty, consistency and chaos. Often, these opposing experiences exist side by side, and that complexity can be confusing, even contradictory. You may find yourself loving a foster parent who also hurt you, missing a home that never truly felt safe, or carrying gratitude for a meal or a birthday alongside grief for everything else. These contradictions aren't a mistake. They're human, and they tell the story of adaptation, survival, and resilience under circumstances that rarely made sense.

The difficulty with complexity is that it often feels destabilizing. Humans crave coherence. We want to assign experiences to "good" or "bad," heroes or villains, safe or unsafe. But foster care often breaks those binaries. A caregiver may have fed you, dressed you, and tucked you in, but still emotionally neglected or betrayed your trust. The brain struggles to integrate these opposing experiences, creating a tension that can follow you into adulthood. You may feel guilt for loving someone who hurt you, shame for missing a person who wasn't safe, or confusion over why your gratitude coexists with anger.

This emotional paradox is natural and even necessary. It reflects the nuanced reality of growing up in unpredictable systems. Your nervous system learned to navigate contradictions constantly. You had to parse micro-expressions, decipher moods, and predict instability while still performing gratitude or obedience.

Making Sense Of It
The Patchwork Quilt of Experience

This constant tension taught you adaptability — a skill that is remarkable, even if it left traces of uncertainty in your adult self.

One way to make peace with these contradictions is to view your experiences like a patchwork quilt. Each patch — each memory, each person, each place — carries a different texture and color. Some are soft, comforting, and warm. Others are rough, torn, or sharp. All of them exist together to form a whole. The quilt is not uniform, and it doesn't need to be. Its value is in the way disparate pieces coexist, stitched together by survival, endurance, and adaptation. Recognizing your story as a quilt allows you to hold multiple truths simultaneously: gratitude and grief, love and anger, relief and fear.

The scars you carry — emotional, relational, even physical — are evidence of this patchwork life. They are not stains or weaknesses; they are markers of resilience, proof that you survived complexity that most people never have to face. Some scars are visible, others invisible, but all shape the texture of your inner quilt. Your nervous system remembers them. Your emotions remember them. And by acknowledging them without judgment, you begin to reclaim agency over the story they tell.

Making Sense Of It
The Patchwork Quilt of Experience

Holding space for the entire quilt — the good, the bad, and the scars — is an act of self-compassion. It allows your nervous system to relax its constant vigilance. It allows your mind to move from forced categorization toward integration. It allows your heart to experience tenderness for yourself and for others, even those who caused pain. And it allows your adult self to recognize that your story, in all its complexity, is valid, worthy, and complete in its own way.

Ultimately, it comes down to honoring dualities. Life isn't neatly divided into heroes and villains, safe and unsafe, right and wrong. Your foster care experiences were often messy, contradictory, and human. By allowing yourself to witness and name all of it — the kindness and the harm, the safety and the fear — you reclaim the authority to hold your experiences on your own terms. Your quilt is yours to acknowledge, care for, and integrate, patch by patch, without any shame or apologies.

What did I learn about love from my foster families — and what do I still carry from that?

Were you taught that love had to be earned, stayed unpredictable, or came with strings? What messages are still playing out in your adult relationships?

What did I learn about love from my foster families — and what do I still carry from that?

Was there anyone who made me feel seen or safe — even briefly?

Name them. Let yourself remember that moment. What did they do differently? What did that give you, even if it didn't last?

Was there anyone who made me feel seen or safe — even briefly?

What kind of hurt still lives in me from those years — and have I ever been able to speak it out loud?

Write without censoring. Let your pain, confusion, or betrayal come forward. No one needs to approve your story for it to be real.

What kind of hurt still lives in me from those years — and have I ever been able to speak it out loud?

Did I ever feel like a burden in someone else's home?

Explore what that brought up for you then, and how it might still shape your self-worth now.

Did I ever feel like a burden in someone else's home?

Have I ever felt guilty for being angry at someone who also helped me?

This is a chance to let both things exist side by side. You are allowed to grieve and appreciate — at the same time.

Have I ever felt guilty for being angry at someone who also helped me?

What does "healthy caregiving" mean to me now?

If you were designing it from scratch — no templates, no past — what would safety, support, and love actually look like?

What does "healthy caregiving" mean to me now?

What would I say to my younger self about what happened in those homes?

Let this be a moment of truth-telling and reassurance. That version of you is still listening.

What would I say to my younger self about what happened in those homes?

TRACING THE TRUTH

THE DUALITY JOURNAL

Foster care experiences often live in tension: love and hurt, safety and fear, gratitude and grief. This exercise helps you explore these dualities, allowing you to hold seemingly opposite feelings side by side without judgment. It's a way to witness your full experience and reclaim emotional authority over your story.

Why it helps:
The Duality Journal allows conflicting emotions to coexist safely on paper, validating your nervous system's complex responses. By giving space to both positive and negative experiences, you reduce shame, confusion, and emotional fragmentation. This practice strengthens self-compassion, integration, and recognition of nuance, showing you that it is possible to love, grieve, and honor your experiences all at once. Over time, it fosters balance and helps you carry the full quilt of your life with awareness, presence, and acceptance.

List memories, people, or experiences under each column, noting emotions they evoke.
Write a reflection: "I can feel both __ and __, and it is valid."
Revisit periodically to see patterns, growth, or shifts in perception.

TRACING THE TRUTH

THE DUALITY JOURNAL

| The Good | The Bad |

TRACING THE TRUTH

THE DUALITY JOURNAL

TRACING THE TRUTH

SCARS AND STARS

Scars carry stories — of pain endured, lessons learned, and survival accomplished. Some are visible, others hidden. This exercise transforms your scars into guiding stars, helping you honor the strength embedded in your history and recognize the wisdom your body and heart carry.

Why it helps:
Naming your scars and attaching meaning to them externalizes trauma while highlighting resilience. This shifts the nervous system from shame and tension toward acknowledgment and empowerment. By seeing strength and wisdom in the places that once hurt, you integrate difficult experiences into a coherent narrative. The exercise validates complexity, reduces internal conflict, and fosters a sense of agency, reminding you that your story, with all its contradictions, is both real and worthy of honor.

On a page, draw or list the "scars" you carry — emotional, relational, or physical.
Next to each scar, write the lesson, resilience, or strength it represents.
Place a star or symbol next to each one to honor the survival it signifies.
Reflect on how these stars guide your present choices or sense of self.

TRACING THE TRUTH

SCARS AND STARS

TRACING THE TRUTH

YOUR QUILT OF EXPERIENCE

Your life in foster care is like a quilt made from many different patches — some soft and warm, others rough or jagged. This exercise helps you map and honor those patches, acknowledging that even the parts that hurt or confused you are part of your story. By seeing the whole quilt laid out, you can hold gratitude, grief, love, and anger together — without judgment or forced explanations.

Why it helps:
The act of giving each memory or person a visible space validates all experiences, helping integrate gratitude, grief, love, and anger into a coherent narrative. Over time, the quilt becomes a tangible representation of survival and resilience — a reminder that your story, in all its messy beauty, belongs to you and can be held gently without judgment.

Draw a large quilt shape or use squares/patches on paper.
Label each patch with a memory, person, or experience — both positive and negative.
Color, shade, or decorate each patch to reflect its emotional texture.
Reflect on how the patches interact, noticing contrasts, patterns, and the overall whole.

TRACING THE TRUTH

YOUR QUILT OF EXPERIENCE

TRACING THE TRUTH

YOUR QUILT OF EXPERIENCE

SECTION SEVEN

Facing What the System Took

Questions you learned to swallow. And a system — made of caseworkers, policies, courtrooms, files, and strangers — that tried to fit your life into a paper folder.

This section is for the part of you that still wants to scream, or collapse, or ask "Why did no one fight for me?" Maybe you've tried to be grateful. Maybe you've told yourself it could've been worse. But that doesn't undo the truth: you were a child. And the system should have done better.

Here, you get to be honest. About what was stolen. What was never protected. What you never got to grieve. This chapter isn't about blame — it's about naming. Because healing doesn't come from pretending everything was fine. It comes from finally telling the truth — even when it's messy, angry, or heartbreakingly sad.

Making Sense Of It
The Ledger of Loss

Foster care isn't just a collection of placements or paperwork. It's a system that interacts with a human life in ways both visible and invisible, often leaving gaps that are impossible to ignore. When you look back, it may feel like someone kept a ledger of your life — counting what you did, what you survived, what rules you broke, and what they "allowed" — while the real losses went unrecorded. The system measured compliance and paperwork, not grief, not trauma, not love. And so, what was stolen — time, safety, family connection, cultural roots, identity — often never got acknowledgment.

Part of the pain of facing what the system took is realizing that these losses were not just moments, but structural. They were built into the way the system operated: the hurried caseworker, the ill-fitted foster home, the placement that ended abruptly, the policy that ignored your needs. You might remember hearing phrases like, "It's not that bad" or "Be grateful you have a bed," while the complexity of your experience was brushed aside. And perhaps you internalized these messages — learning to minimize your losses, hide your anger, or measure your worth by survival alone.

Acknowledging what was taken does not mean you are weak or bitter. It is an act of reclamation. By naming the absences, gaps, and injustices, you reclaim your story from the cold, impersonal system that tried to define it for you.

Making Sense Of It
The Ledger of Loss

Naming what was lost also helps your nervous system understand what is real, giving the body permission to release tension, grief, and the lingering hypervigilance that comes from surviving a system that failed to protect you.

Another layer is recognizing the emotional theft: the stolen trust, the stolen childhood, the stolen relationships. These losses are often invisible to others, because the system never recognized them either. You may carry longing for connections that were cut off prematurely, rage at missed protections, or sadness for moments you were too young to articulate. These emotions are valid. They were never unearned, even if the world tried to tell you otherwise.

Facing these losses also allows you to see the paradox of survival. You were often forced to grow up too quickly, to become self-reliant in environments where dependency is expected. You may have developed resilience, cunning, or independence, but these came at a cost: the things the system failed to provide. Understanding this paradox is essential to untangling guilt or shame that you may feel for surviving when the system fell short. It's not about blaming yourself — it's about holding space for the truth.

Making Sense Of It
The Ledger of Loss

The process of confronting these systemic losses is deeply empowering. It allows you to measure your own life outside of the ledger the system tried to keep. You begin to name what was stolen, grieve it, and reclaim agency over what remains. This is not a theoretical exercise; it is practical nervous system repair. Naming absence, loss, and injustice signals safety to your body, shows your mind that your story matters, and validates feelings that may have been silenced for decades.

Ultimately, facing what the system took is about reclaiming authority over your narrative. You give yourself permission to feel, to rage, to mourn, to cry, and to reflect — without apology, judgment, or minimization. The system may have been inadequate, careless, or even harmful, but you are not inadequate. You are the holder of your own story, and by naming the truths that were ignored, you take your first steps toward claiming the life and sense of self that was always yours to shape.

What was taken from me that I never got to grieve?

Time, safety, identity, siblings, birthdays, innocence — name every piece of your story that felt stolen or discarded.

What was taken from me that I never got to grieve?

What would I say if I could speak honestly to "the system"?

Write the unsaid. The rage. The betrayal. The disappointment. Let yourself speak directly, without censoring.

What would I say if I could speak honestly to "the system"?

When did I feel voiceless — and what did I wish someone had done or said for me?

This is your chance to write the justice you needed. To witness your own abandonment with compassion.

When did I feel voiceless — and what did I wish someone had done or said for me?

Who told me I was "resilient" when what I really needed was help?

Explore how survival became expected, and what it cost you to keep pushing through.

Who told me I was "resilient" when what I really needed was help?

Where does my anger live in my body — and what happens when I try to name it?

Let your body speak. Describe the sensations. Is it heat, tightness, shaking, numbness? Where does it go when you give it permission?

Where does my anger live in my body — and what happens when I try to name it?

What do I still feel is "too much" to say out loud?

This prompt is your permission slip. Nothing is too intense here. Your truth is welcome.

What do I still feel is "too much" to say out loud?

What do I wish someone had told me when I entered the system?

Write the words you needed. The ones that could've changed something — even if no one said them then, you can say them now.

What do I wish someone had told me when I entered the system?

TRACING THE TRUTH

THE LEDGER

Imagine the system as a ledger that kept track of compliance, placements, and paperwork — but ignored what really mattered: your grief, your needs, your losses. This exercise allows you to create your own ledger, one that lists the things taken from you, so that your life and losses are finally acknowledged on your terms. By naming these absences, you reclaim agency and validate what the system ignored.

Why it helps:
Writing your own ledger externalizes invisible systemic losses, giving them recognition that was denied. It allows your nervous system to track, process, and release tension from unacknowledged grief. The exercise validates your experiences, reduces internalized shame, and reinforces agency. By naming what was stolen, you reclaim authorship of your story and create a container for complex emotions — anger, grief, and sadness — that the system ignored. Over time, this practice strengthens self-trust and allows you to carry the memory of loss without letting it define or limit your life.

Fill in the rows with placements, relationships, opportunities, or protections you were denied.
Reflect on patterns or recurring losses, noticing emotions that arise.
Close by affirming: "I see my losses. They mattered. My story matters."

TRACING THE TRUTH

THE LEDGER

What Was Taken	How It Affected Me	What I Needed

TRACING THE TRUTH

LETTER TO THE SYSTEM

The system may never have offered accountability, apology, or recognition. Writing a letter allows you to express what you could not safely express before — anger, grief, questions, or truth — without needing a response. This is about witnessing your own story and reclaiming authority over it.

Why it helps:
This exercise externalizes anger and grief safely, engaging mind, body, and emotion. Naming systemic failures validates your experience and allows your nervous system to release tension carried for years. Even without a response, the act of addressing the system affirms your voice, strengthens self-trust, and reclaims narrative authority. Over time, this practice integrates complex feelings, reduces shame, and supports the healing of wounds left by neglect or oversight, enabling you to carry your story with agency rather than silent burden.

Write a letter to "the system" — foster care, courts, caseworkers, or policy itself.
Include what was taken, what hurt, and what you wish had been different.
Speak your truth fully; there is no need to censor or soften any of it.

TRACING THE TRUTH

LETTER TO THE SYSTEM

TRACING THE TRUTH

LETTER TO THE SYSTEM

TRACING THE TRUTH

LETTER TO THE SYSTEM

TRACING THE TRUTH

LETTER TO THE SYSTEM

ACTION

SEEING THE BIGGER PICTURE

When someone's behavior triggers you—or when you catch yourself blaming yourself—your mind often jumps to the harshest story: "It's all my fault," or "They're deliberately hurting me." Compassionate Reattribution helps you pause and look at the situation more realistically. By considering context, other explanations, and human limits, you can soften blame, see things more fairly, and plan a small step to repair or respond thoughtfully. It doesn't excuse harmful behavior, but it frees your mind from spinning in harsh judgments.

Identify the blamey thought.
Example: "I shouldn't have said that—now they're upset."

Consider other explanations.
Context: maybe they had a rough day.
Skills: maybe they struggle to communicate.
Nervous system: stress can make anyone react sharply.

Choose a fair attribution.
Example: "They were stressed, not necessarily upset at me personally."

Pick one small repair step (if needed).
Example: check in calmly, clarify your intent, or take a pause before responding.

BLAMEY THOUGHT	OTHER EXPLANATIONS	FAIR ATTRIBUTION & REPAIR STEP

ACTION

SEEING THE BIGGER PICTURE

BLAMEY THOUGHT	OTHER EXPLANATIONS	FAIR ATTRIBUTION & REPAIR STEP

ACTION

THE TRIGGER MAP

When you react automatically, it often feels like there's no pause between what happens and how you respond. This exercise helps you slow things down and see the chain of events clearly—what triggered the feeling, the thought that popped up, the urge, and what actually happened. Once you can see it all laid out, you can spot the point where you can intervene next time. That small pause is enough to change the outcome, give yourself more control, and break patterns that have been running on autopilot.

Map the chain: Write down each step in order

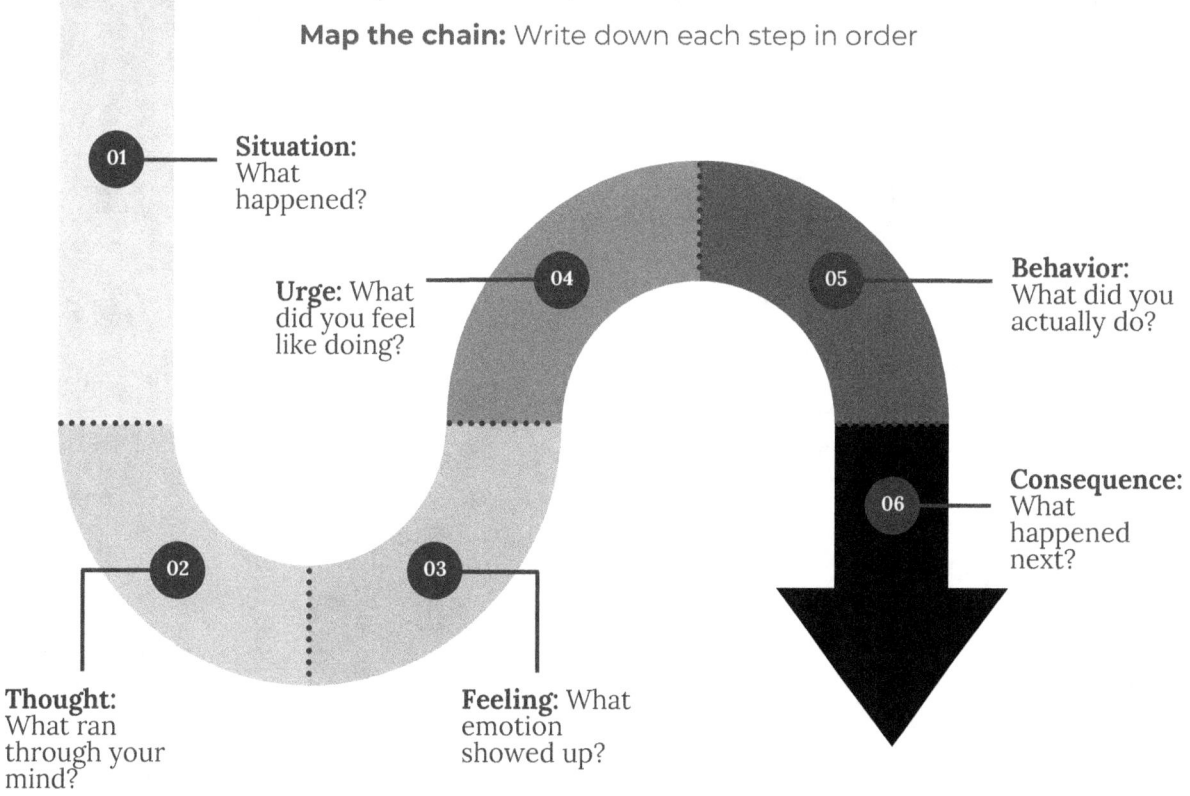

- 01 **Situation:** What happened?
- 02 **Thought:** What ran through your mind?
- 03 **Feeling:** What emotion showed up?
- 04 **Urge:** What did you feel like doing?
- 05 **Behavior:** What did you actually do?
- 06 **Consequence:** What happened next?

Circle your change point. Look at the chain and find the first step where you could intervene next time.

Plan one interruption. Pick a tool or skill to use—like a short breathing exercise, a script you can say, or a grounding move—to pause the chain and respond differently.

SECTION EIGHT

The Inner Child I Still Carry

There's a part of you that never stopped waiting. For someone to come back. For a door to open. For a grown-up to kneel beside you and say, "I'm here. You're safe now."

That part — the foster kid within — isn't gone. They show up in your fears of being left, in how hard you fight to be heard, in the way you sometimes push people away even when you long for connection. You might have learned to call this "immaturity" or "overreacting," but it's not that. It's an inner child who learned survival in a world that didn't protect them.

This section is about returning to that part of you. Not to fix them, but to love them — finally, gently, unconditionally. Because healing isn't just about moving forward. Sometimes it's about turning back, sitting beside the child you were, and saying the words no one ever said to you then: "I've got you now."

Making Sense Of It
Meeting Yourself at the Playground

The inner child is not a metaphor; it is a living presence shaped by survival, waiting patiently for acknowledgment. For adults who grew up in foster care, this child carries the weight of missed protections, fractured attachments, and the unspoken rules of survival. They learned early how to shrink, perform, or disappear to stay safe. They learned to hold grief silently and distrust deeply. Even now, that child sits somewhere inside you — often quietly, sometimes as panic, rage, or sadness — reminding you that the survival strategies you developed came at a cost.

Many adults try to outrun the inner child, pushing feelings of vulnerability aside or labeling them as weakness. You may have learned to call your needs "too much," your emotions "overreactions," or your fears "immaturity." But these are not flaws. They are echoes of survival. That child learned to navigate a world that didn't keep them safe. That child's longing for presence, care, and love is real, valid, and deeply human.

Returning to your inner child is not about regression or self-indulgence. It is about witness, validation, and connection. It is about sitting beside the part of you that never got to feel safe and offering the protection, compassion, and acknowledgement that was denied. This process does not erase the past, but it helps integrate it into the adult self, allowing both to coexist with honesty, dignity, and care.

Making Sense Of It
Meeting Yourself at the Playground

The inner child may carry conflicting emotions. You may notice anger at the world for failing you, sadness for what was stolen, and longing for connections that never materialized. These feelings may appear in moments of intimacy, conflict, or loss, often triggered by events that echo past neglect. Meeting the child within means noticing these triggers without judgment, leaning in to curiosity rather than avoidance, and learning to respond with compassion rather than shame.

Physiologically, connecting with your inner child is a form of nervous system repair. For decades, your body may have been primed for vigilance, bracing for harm that never came or had already passed. By intentionally offering safety and comfort to the child within, you create a new template for relational safety. You train your nervous system to feel seen, heard, and protected — conditions that were once absent. Over time, this rewiring fosters resilience, emotional regulation, and a stronger sense of self.

This work is delicate. The inner child may resist at first, frightened of being disappointed again. They may test your boundaries, retreat, or demand attention in ways that feel inconvenient or uncomfortable. These behaviors are not failures; they are attempts to communicate needs that were never met. Approaching with patience and presence — even in small doses — sends the message that this child is no longer alone, that someone is here to bear witness and offer care.

Making Sense Of It
Meeting Yourself at the Playground

Healing with your inner child is not linear. Some days will feel tender and connected; others, raw and resistant. Some memories will surface gently; others will hit with the intensity of long-held pain. The goal is not perfection or immediate resolution. It is to establish a relationship rooted in acknowledgment, empathy, and trust — showing yourself, finally, that your needs are valid and that the survival strategies of your youth no longer define your worth or capacity for love.

Ultimately, sitting beside your inner child is an act of reclamation. It affirms that you are not defined solely by trauma or survival. It teaches that compassion — first for yourself, then for others — begins with recognition of the child who always waited. It creates a bridge between past and present, fostering integration, safety, and a deepened sense of belonging within your own life.

What did the child version of me never get to feel?

Let your younger self speak — the one who had to grow up fast or shut down to survive. What feelings were pushed down?

What did the child version of me never get to feel?

When I think about my childhood, what memory still holds the most emotional weight?

Choose one moment that your body or heart still reacts to. Write from inside it — what did you need that you didn't get?

When I think about my childhood, what memory still holds the most emotional weight?

What survival strategies did I develop as a foster kid that I still carry today?

Hyper-independence, emotional numbness, people-pleasing — name the ways you learned to adapt, and honor their wisdom.

What survival strategies did I develop as a foster kid that I still carry today?

What did I secretly hope a caregiver would say to me back then?

Write it out now. Word for word. As if they finally said it, and meant it.

What did I secretly hope a caregiver would say to me back then?

What does my inner child need from me today?

Maybe it's rest. Maybe it's comfort, or protection, or play. Let that younger part of you speak through the page.

What does my inner child need from me today?

Where does that part of me show up in my adult life?

Notice your reactions — the moments when you feel smaller, scared, or like you're "too much." What is your inner child asking for in those moments?

Where does that part of me show up in my adult life?

If I could speak to the child I was, what would I want them to know now?

This is your letter to them. Write it from the heart. Let it be a turning point.

If I could speak to the child I was, what would I want them to know now?

ACTION

QUICK ANCHORS

When a trigger hits, your brain often goes on autopilot—stress, worry, or old patterns take over before you can respond intentionally. This exercise can give you a quick, tangible anchor. By having a short reminder of a helpful thought and concrete actions ready, you can interrupt the automatic response and respond in a way that actually supports you. Keeping it close—literally in your hand, pocket, or on your desk—makes it accessible exactly when you need it most.

On the card on the left: Write a common trigger + a supportive, grounding thought.
Example: Trigger: "Feeling ignored in a conversation." Helpful thought: "I can pause and breathe before reacting."

On the card on the right: List 3 concrete action steps you can take and one support contact.
Example Actions: Take 3 deep breaths, step away for 2 minutes, write down your feelings. Support contact: text a trusted friend.

Return to these regularly.
Use it. Refer to them when you notice triggers. Practice until it becomes second nature.

Triggers & Grounding Thought	Action Steps & Support Contact

ACTION

QUICK ANCHORS

Triggers & Grounding Thought

Action Steps & Support Contact

SECTION NINE

Rebuilding Safety

Safety isn't a concept — it's a felt sense. It's what your body knows before your mind can explain it. And if you spent years in foster care, or bouncing between homes, or never feeling truly wanted, safety might not be something you've ever fully experienced. Or if you did, it may not have lasted.

This section is about relearning what it means to feel safe — not just in your environment, but in your skin. In your relationships. In your breath. In the way you hold yourself. Because after trauma, even goodness can feel dangerous. Love can feel suspicious. Calm can feel like the prelude to chaos.

You don't have to force trust. You don't have to push yourself to be "open." Safety is built in small moments — gentle rhythms of consistency, choice, and presence. And you get to go at your own pace. Rebuilding safety isn't weak. It's sacred. It's how healing begins to take root.

Making Sense Of It
Safety as a Felt Sense

Safety isn't an abstract idea. It isn't a checklist or a concept to memorize. Safety is felt — first in the body, then in the mind. For adults who grew up in foster care, safety may have been fleeting, conditional, or entirely absent. Perhaps it arrived in bursts: a clean bed, a kind word, a meal — only to be withdrawn without explanation. Perhaps the very environment you needed to breathe freely was unpredictable, judgmental, or even threatening. Over time, your nervous system learned to brace, scan, and anticipate danger before your mind could even catch up. Safety became a distant or imagined state, not a lived reality.

To relearn safety, you must begin with the body. Trauma teaches the nervous system to assume threat as default; it becomes hypervigilant, tense, and primed to protect. When safety is inconsistent or absent, your body carries the memory of danger long after the environment has changed. This means that even in calm, loving, or supportive situations, you may feel anxiety, distrust, or an urge to flee. Your mind might say, "It's fine," but your body knows otherwise. Healing begins when the body is given permission to sense safety again, moment by moment, gesture by gesture, breath by breath.

Imagine safety as a garden. At first, the soil may be rocky, overgrown with weeds, or scorched from neglect. Tiny seeds — trust, presence, calm — can be planted, but they need consistent care. You cannot force them to bloom. You water gently, remove debris, and notice small sprouts emerging.

Making Sense Of It
Safety as a Felt Sense

Over time, those sprouts grow stronger, eventually creating a space where the body can rest, where breath deepens, and where relationships can be approached without constant vigilance. This metaphor isn't sentimental — it's practical: nervous systems respond to gradual, repeated signals that the world is not unsafe.

Safety also exists in the rhythms of life, not just events. Predictable routines, consistent self-care, reliable relationships, and honoring boundaries all signal safety to the body. These rhythms teach your nervous system that calm doesn't mean danger is imminent, and presence doesn't mean abandonment is around the corner. You learn to inhabit your skin without armor, to exhale without bracing, and to receive care without calculating its withdrawal.

It's important to recognize that safety is deeply personal. What feels safe to one person may not feel safe to another. For some, it is physical space; for others, it is emotional attunement, boundaries that are honored, or simply having a choice in what happens next. Safety is also incremental. A single moment of trust may feel insignificant, yet it is a brick in the foundation of a nervous system that has been primed for unpredictability. Each small experience accumulates, teaching your body, heart, and mind that safety is not a fantasy, but a felt reality. Safety doesn't erase past harm, but it allows healing to take root. When the body learns that calm is not always followed by chaos, that love is not always conditional, and that your presence matters, you begin to reclaim agency.

What does safety feel like to me — physically, emotionally, relationally?

Go beyond the idea of safety. What does your body actually feel when you are truly safe? Warmth? Ease? Freedom?

What does safety feel like to me — physically, emotionally, relationally?

When have I felt safest in my life?

Look for moments — even small ones — when you felt truly held, grounded, or at peace. Describe what was present.

When have I felt safest in my life?

Where in my body do I carry a sense of unsafety?

Get curious about tension, tightness, or restlessness. These may be places your body stores the imprint of unsafety.

Where in my body do I carry a sense of unsafety?

What does my nervous system need when I'm triggered or shut down?

Reflect on patterns — do you tend to fight, flee, freeze, or fawn? What helps you return to center?

What does my nervous system need when I'm triggered or shut down?

Who or what do I want to trust... but struggle to?

Is there a relationship, situation, or part of yourself you long to trust — but your system says "no"? What does that part need?

Who or what do I want to trust... but struggle to?

What boundaries help me feel safer in connection?

Boundaries aren't walls. They're bridges with doors. What limits help you feel emotionally protected and open to real closeness?

What boundaries help me feel safer in connection?

Safety is a birthright — not something you have to earn. And even if no one ever taught you how to feel safe, it's not too late to learn.

ACTION

CRISIS PAUSE

When emotions run high, it's easy to get pulled into extremes—either reacting purely from feelings or overthinking with logic alone. Wise Mind Access helps you pause and bring both sides together: your emotional insight and your reasoned perspective. By visualizing Emotion Mind and Reasonable Mind meeting, you create space for clarity, calm, and grounded decision-making. Writing down the first calm thought that arises captures the guidance of your "middle path," helping you respond intentionally rather than reacting impulsively.

STEP 1

Stop.

Freeze for a beat. Don't send the text, don't make the call, don't decide. Hands still.

STEP 2

Take a step back.

One slow breath or a literal step backward. Say quietly, "Pause."

STEP 3

Observe.

Notice: What's happening in my body? What are the facts (not the story)? What's my goal? What's in my control right now? (This is your Reasonable Mind check.)

STEP 4

Proceed mindfully.

Pick one effective action that serves your goal—something small, safe, and workable (e.g., "wait 10 minutes," "use a calm script," "walk to the sink and drink water"). Follow through.

S T

ACTION

SPEAK & STAY STEADY

When emotions run high, it's easy to either go silent or come in too strong. DEAR MAN gives you a clear framework for making requests—or saying no—without guilt or aggression. It balances honesty with effectiveness so you can be heard and respected, even in difficult conversations.

Describe

Briefly state the facts. ("Last week, you didn't follow through on picking up the kids.")

Express

Share how it impacted you. ("I felt really stressed and overwhelmed.")

Assert

Clearly ask for what you need. ("I need you to confirm pick-up times in advance.")

Reinforce

Show the positive outcome. ("That way, we both have more peace of mind.")

Mindful

Stay on point; don't chase distractions or get pulled into side arguments.

Appear confident

Sit up, steady tone, eye contact if possible. Confidence helps your words land.

Negotiate

Be flexible; invite collaboration. ("If that time doesn't work, let's pick another together.")

SECTION TEN

Anger, Grief, and the System That Let Me Down

You weren't crazy. You weren't "too much." You were reacting to what happened — or what didn't happen when it should have. The foster care system, for many, promised safety but delivered something far more complicated. Maybe you bounced between homes like baggage. Maybe people said "this is for your good," while your heart broke silently in rooms you didn't choose.

And maybe there's a rage inside you — or a grief so wide it feels like it could swallow you. This section is for that. For the tears that never came. For the scream that stayed locked in your chest. For the justice you didn't get.

You don't have to forgive the system. You don't have to pretend it wasn't harmful. But you do deserve to name what was never fair, to feel what you had to numb, and to begin reclaiming your power — one honest feeling at a time.

Making Sense Of It

The Fire and the Flood

Anger and grief are not problems to be fixed. For adults who grew up in foster care, these emotions are truth-tellers — signals that something vital was taken, overlooked, or denied. The system promised care but often delivered chaos, indifference, or harm. You were a child navigating placements, policies, and adults who were themselves constrained or indifferent. Your anger and grief are the body's natural responses to those betrayals. They are the echoes of experiences too intense, too unfair, and too complex to fit into neat categories.

Anger in foster care is often misunderstood. You may have been labeled "difficult," "aggressive," or "too much" for reacting to circumstances beyond your control. But anger is not misbehavior. It is a compass pointing toward injustice, toward boundaries violated, toward needs ignored. Every flash of rage — every moment of frustration or resentment — has a story behind it, and that story deserves acknowledgment. Anger is the body's way of saying: This mattered. I mattered. I am here.

Grief is its twin, though quieter for some. Grief is the weight of absence, loss, and unfulfilled longing: parents who couldn't protect you, siblings you rarely saw, homes that never felt like home. Grief does not always arrive neatly; it can hide under sarcasm, numbness, perfectionism, or even hyper-independence. The system may have taught you to minimize grief, to smile despite pain, to pretend survival was enough. But grief doesn't disappear because it is inconvenient or invisible. It waits patiently inside, sometimes surfacing unexpectedly in memories, triggers, or relationships.

Making Sense Of It
The Fire and the Flood

One reason anger and grief feel overwhelming is that they are often tangled. Anger at the system may trigger grief for what was lost; grief may ignite anger at those who failed to protect you. Both are tied to your nervous system's survival wiring. Chronic stress, hypervigilance, and the constant adaptation required in foster care shape how these emotions show up. You may feel them in your chest, your stomach, your jaw, or in moments when your adult life seems "normal" but your body remembers.

Acknowledging anger and grief is not about indulgence; it is about reclaiming agency. Naming what was unfair, cruel, or absent allows your nervous system to stop carrying it unprocessed. It signals to your mind and body that these responses are valid, and that your experience matters. It's a first step toward integrating the trauma of the past with the adult self, creating a bridge between survival strategies and intentional emotional regulation.

Another truth is that anger and grief are inherently reparative. Expressed safely, they reclaim parts of your voice that were silenced. They assert boundaries and reinforce self-worth. They allow you to witness your own suffering without judgment, transforming raw emotional energy into insight, action, and self-protection. They are tools of empowerment rather than indicators of weakness.

What am I still angry about — even if I've never admitted it out loud?

Let the truth come through. You don't need to fix it or justify it. Just name it.

What am I still angry about — even if I've never admitted it out loud?

Who failed me, and what did I need them to do instead?

Anger often hides under unmet needs. What would it have looked like if someone had shown up how you needed?

Who failed me, and what did I need them to do instead?

What grief do I carry about what the system took from me — or couldn't protect?

Grief isn't only about death. It's about absence, silence, confusion. What are you still mourning?

What grief do I carry about what the system took from me — or couldn't protect?

Have I ever turned my anger inward? What has that cost me?

Sometimes we blame ourselves for what was never ours to carry. What happens when you let that blame go?

Have I ever turned my anger inward? What has that cost me?

What part of me is afraid to feel this anger — and why?

There may be younger parts who associate anger with danger or rejection. Get curious. Reassure them.

What part of me is afraid to feel this anger — and why?

If I could say one uncensored thing to the system, or the people who hurt me, what would I say?

Give yourself permission to say it. No edits. No guilt.

If I could say one uncensored thing to the system, or the people who hurt me, what would I say?

TRACING THE TRUTH

THE FIRE JAR

Anger is energy that wants acknowledgment and expression. This exercise allows you to capture your rage in a safe, contained way — honoring it without harming yourself or others. By giving it a symbolic container, you can observe, release, and reclaim the power of your emotions.

Why it helps:
The Fire Jar externalizes anger, giving the nervous system a safe channel to release energy. Naming and symbolically containing rage reduces overwhelm, fosters self-regulation, and signals to the body that these emotions are valid and witnessed. The act of release allows empowerment and control over feelings that were once dictated by a system that failed you. Over time, it transforms anger from a reactive force into a conscious, contained, and healing energy — strengthening agency, clarity, and self-trust.

Find a jar, cup, or container.
Write down what makes you angry — injustices, betrayals, system failures — on slips of paper.
Place each slip in the jar, imagining the energy being contained safely.
When ready, tear, or discard the notes, feeling the release of pent-up anger.

ACTION

FEEL IT, DON'T FEED IT

Neuroscience shows that most emotions, if left alone, rise, crest, and fall within about 90 seconds. What keeps us trapped is the story we add — the rumination, replaying, and self-criticism. The 90-Second Emotion Wave helps you move through the raw sensation without getting stuck in the mental loops that amplify pain. By anchoring your attention to your breath and gently offering your body comfort, you allow the emotion to pass through instead of drowning in it. This teaches you that emotions are temporary visitors, not permanent truths.

Set a timer for 90 seconds.

Notice the emotion rise. Imagine it as a wave building. Stay with the body sensations.

Anchor with breath. Breathe slowly, lengthening your exhale. Place a hand where the emotion feels strongest in your body.

Ride the crest. Let the feeling peak without pushing it away or fueling it.

Allow the fall. As the wave settles, ask yourself softly: "What do I need now?"

ACTION

KIND INTENTION SETTING

Intentions are like a quiet compass. They don't pressure you or set you up to "succeed" or "fail." They just give you something gentle to return to when the day gets noisy. Starting your morning with one small sentence helps you set the tone: maybe you want to be steadier, softer, braver. Ending the day with another sentence helps you notice where you actually showed up, without the self-punishment. It's less about performance and more about self-trust — proof that you can guide yourself kindly, one day at a time.

Morning: Write one line — "Today, I will show up with ___." (e.g., patience, presence, steadiness).

Carry it lightly: Let it sit in the back of your mind; check in when you feel pulled off course.

Evening: Write one line — "Today, I showed up with ___." Be honest, but kind.

Close the loop: Let the day go. Tomorrow is fresh.

SECTION ELEVEN

Love, Connection, and the People Who Tried

Sometimes, in the middle of the pain, there were glimmers of kindness. A foster parent who stayed up with you when you had nightmares. A teacher who believed in you. A social worker who genuinely tried. It's okay to remember those moments — not because they erase what was hard, but because your heart also needs the space to remember what was good.

Maybe that love was messy. Maybe it came too late, or didn't stay long enough. Maybe you're still not sure how to hold gratitude and anger at the same time. That's okay. This isn't about forcing forgiveness or minimizing the hurt. It's about allowing your story to be big enough to hold both — the wounds and the warmth.

Love in the system isn't simple. But you're allowed to feel it all. You're allowed to say: "They tried. And it still hurt." Both can be true. And both deserve your voice.

Making Sense Of It
The Glass Half-Full, Half-Held

Even in foster care, even in fractured homes, love finds a way in. Not perfect love. Not steady, consistent, or fully reliable. But small gestures, fleeting moments, and rare connections leave traces in the heart. A teacher who noticed your effort, a foster parent who tucked you in, a caseworker who actually listened — these moments matter. They do not erase the neglect, the pain, or the chaos. They coexist with it, like sunlight breaking through a stormy sky. And honoring them does not diminish the losses you endured. In fact, it helps integrate the full spectrum of your experience.

For many adults who lived through foster care, the instinct may be to deny or minimize these glimmers of care. Maybe you were taught to focus on survival, to protect yourself from disappointment, or to distrust the intentions of adults. Remembering love can feel dangerous — like opening a door that will slam shut. And yet, acknowledging the people who tried allows you to notice that goodness existed, however fleeting, and that your heart was capable of receiving care, even in small doses.

This section is not about gratitude as a moral obligation. You are not required to forgive, to feel indebted, or to diminish your pain. Instead, it is about holding complexity: seeing the kindness without excusing the harm. The nervous system responds to relational safety, even temporary, imperfect safety. These moments teach your body that warmth is possible, that attention can be given, and that your needs are not inherently burdensome. Even when love was inconsistent, these traces leave physiological and emotional imprints that can be nourished in adulthood.

Making Sense Of It
The Glass Half-Full, Half-Held

Think of these experiences as a glass both half-full and half-held. Half-full because someone genuinely tried. Half-held because it was limited, incomplete, or inconsistent. Holding both truths simultaneously allows you to reclaim your narrative — to acknowledge that pain and care can coexist. It trains the nervous system to tolerate complexity, reduces the tendency toward black-and-white thinking, and cultivates the ability to feel gratitude and grief without shame.

It's also a chance to reclaim agency. In foster care, much of life was decided for you: placements, rules, schedules, and expectations. Recognizing the people who tried lets you name what mattered to you — a choice you may not have felt you could make as a child. You get to decide what counts as meaningful, what leaves an imprint, and how to carry it forward. You are learning to honor not only what was withheld but also what was offered, even imperfectly.

Finally, holding these moments opens the heart to adult relational possibilities. Many adults who grew up in foster care struggle with intimacy or trust because early love was inconsistent. By gently recognizing that love could exist, even in fractured forms, you give yourself permission to believe it can exist now — in friends, partners, mentors, and chosen family. This doesn't erase caution or trauma-informed boundaries; it complements them. It allows your nervous system to integrate hope with wisdom, and warmth with discernment.

Who are the people I remember with warmth — even if things were still hard?

Name them. Let the nuance live. You can hold that they tried, even if it wasn't enough.

Who are the people I remember with warmth — even if things were still hard?

What moments of kindness or connection still stay with me?

Even small gestures — a meal, a word, a glance — can leave a lasting imprint. Let those memories rise.

What moments of kindness or connection still stay with me?

Is there a part of me that feels guilty for feeling grateful?

Sometimes survivors struggle to hold positive memories because they think it invalidates the pain. Explore what's underneath that.

Is there a part of me that feels guilty for feeling grateful?

What did I learn about love from the people who tried?

Love can be healing, but also complicated. What messages did you absorb — and are those messages still helping you?

What did I learn about love from the people who tried?

What would I want to say to someone who tried to love me — honestly and without censorship?

Write it like a letter. Include the good and the painful. Let it be messy.

What would I want to say to someone who tried to love me — honestly and without censorship?

How do I carry those "good moments" in my body? Do I allow myself to feel them?

Sometimes trauma makes even joy feel unsafe. Where do those memories live in your body?

How do I carry those "good moments" in my body? Do I allow myself to feel them?

ACTION

PROTECTIVE BUBBLE

When emotions run high or interactions feel draining, it's easy for your energy to get scattered. Imagining a soft, light bubble around you helps create a sense of personal space and safety. Using your breath to strengthen the bubble on the inhale and filter in only what feels nourishing on the exhale trains your nervous system to notice boundaries, giving you a calm, centered feeling even in challenging situations.

Sit or stand comfortably, spine tall.

Visualize a soft bubble surrounding your body, glowing lightly.

Inhale and imagine the bubble strengthening, expanding slightly.

Exhale and let in only what nourishes — warmth, safety, or calm.

Continue for 1–3 minutes, noticing a sense of energetic protection and centeredness.

You don't have to throw out the good to validate the hard. You can love someone and still feel hurt by them. You can hold gratitude without forgetting what they couldn't give. That's emotional maturity

ACTION

SOFT EYES RESET

When we're anxious or hypervigilant, our gaze often narrows, making the world feel tense or threatening. Softening your eyes and expanding your peripheral vision sends a signal to your nervous system that it's safe to relax. This subtle shift can reduce tension in the shoulders, jaw, and chest, helping you feel steadier and more grounded, even in moments of stress.

Sit or stand comfortably with spine tall.

Focus softly ahead, allowing your peripheral vision to widen.

Notice objects to the sides without staring directly at them.

Pay attention to how your body responds — shoulders, jaw, and breath may soften naturally.

Continue for 1–2 minutes, gently returning your focus to soft vision whenever it narrows.

SECTION TWELVE

Parenting Myself Now – Healing the Abandonment Wound

If you were moved through homes, left without explanations, or simply never had someone stay long enough to show you you mattered, abandonment may have left its fingerprint on everything — how you love, how you trust, even how you breathe when things get quiet.

It's not just the moment of being left. It's the long, echoing silence afterward. The waiting. The wondering what you did wrong. The belief that love always leaves. But here's what's true now: you are no longer helpless. You are no longer voiceless. You may still carry wounds, but you also carry power — the power to turn toward the self who was abandoned and say: I will not leave you.

This isn't easy work. But it's sacred. It's the slow, steady return to yourself. And it begins here, with gentle reparenting, fierce compassion, and the brave decision to become someone who stays.

Making Sense Of It
The Keeper of the Small Self

Abandonment is not only a memory — it is a feeling, a lingering pulse in the body that tells you, I might not be safe. I might be left. For adults who grew up in foster care, that pulse often beats quietly, persistently, threading through relationships, self-esteem, and even the rhythm of daily life. It is not a flaw; it is an imprint of survival. When adults were inconsistent, absent, or silent, the nervous system learned to anticipate loss as default. And if your inner child never had someone who stayed, that part of you may still flinch at closeness, still shrink in the face of care, still carry a quiet but insistent question: Will you leave too?

Reparenting yourself begins with acknowledgment. It is about stepping into the role your caregivers never could — the one who shows up, who provides consistency, and who bears witness to the small self that once had no advocate. This is not fantasy or indulgence; it is nervous system work, relational repair, and reclamation of agency. By acting as your own steadfast parent, you teach your body and mind that love can exist without conditions, that presence can be chosen, and that abandonment is no longer inevitable.

The process is tender, courageous, and incremental. You may start with small gestures: making space to sit quietly with yourself, offering soothing words when you feel panic or self-criticism, or honoring your needs without guilt. These micro-actions send messages to the nervous system that safety, care, and stability can exist outside of external circumstances.

Making Sense Of It
The Keeper of the Small Self

Over time, they accumulate, forming the foundation of what is called "earned secure attachment" — the lived understanding that you are capable of holding yourself, meeting your needs, and offering a constant presence where it was once absent.

Part of reparenting is noticing and naming the patterns left by abandonment. You might notice hyper-vigilance, over-accommodation in relationships, fear of asking for help, or avoidance of intimacy. You might catch yourself leaving situations preemptively to avoid being left. These responses were adaptive, but now they can be transformed. When you recognize them, you can choose differently — not by erasing pain, but by stepping into a compassionate, steady presence for yourself. You become the adult who stays, even when fear whispers that history will repeat itself.

Healing abandonment also involves dialogue with the inner child — the small self who remembers being unseen or left behind. Speak to them, listen, hold them, and validate what they felt. By repeatedly returning to this practice, you reinforce the truth that presence is now a conscious choice, and that your power no longer depends on someone else's reliability. The nervous system slowly learns that you are a constant, and that the small self can relax, trust, and breathe.

It's essential to hold complexity here: reparenting is not linear, and setbacks do not mean failure. Some days, fear, anger, or sadness may surge. Others, moments of tenderness or comfort may feel fragile. Both experiences are valid.

When did I first learn that people could leave?

Explore the earliest memories of separation or loss — not to re-traumatize, but to honor what your younger self survived.

When did I first learn that people could leave?

What did I make it mean about me when someone left?

Did you believe you were unlovable, forgettable, "too much" or "not enough"? Let those beliefs speak so they can begin to soften.

What did I make it mean about me when someone left?

What would it feel like to stay with myself — even when I feel messy, angry, or ashamed?

Imagine not abandoning yourself in moments you once were abandoned. What does that stir in you?

> What would it feel like to stay with myself — even when I feel messy, angry, or ashamed?

What does the child in me need most right now?

Let your inner child speak. What do they long to hear? To feel? To be told again and again?

What does the child in me need most right now?

What does safety actually look like, sound like, and feel like for me now?

Let your body describe it. Go beyond words. What rhythms, tones, and gestures signal: "You're safe here"?

What does safety actually look like, sound like, and feel like for me now?

Have I ever walked away from myself? How can I begin to return?

This isn't about blame. It's about noticing the moments we leave our own side — and learning how to come back.

Have I ever walked away from myself? How can I begin to return?

TRACING THE TRUTH

THE KEEPER'S LETTER

Your inner child waited for someone who stayed. This exercise helps you step into the role of the adult who is always present — your own steadfast parent. By writing to yourself from this place, you provide the care, consistency, and validation that were once absent.

Why it helps:
This exercise provides the nervous system with repeated, safe signals of presence and care. It rewires attachment patterns, reinforces self-trust, and validates emotions that were once ignored or dismissed. By repeatedly acting as the adult who stays, you strengthen internal consistency, build relational confidence, and integrate past experiences into a coherent narrative of care. Over time, your inner child learns that absence is no longer inevitable, fostering emotional regulation, self-compassion, and the embodied sense that you are held — always — by the adult you have become.

Address a letter to your younger self, using their name or a loving title.
Speak to their fears, acknowledging what was missed or lost.
Promise presence: words like *"I am here. I will stay. You are safe."*
Read the letter aloud or place it somewhere symbolic to revisit when needed.

TRACING THE TRUTH

THE KEEPER'S LETTER

TRACING THE TRUTH

THE KEEPER'S LETTER

TRACING THE TRUTH

THE KEEPER'S LETTER

TRACING THE TRUTH

THE KEEPER'S LETTER

SHELF IT FOR LATER

Sometimes intrusive images or thoughts crash in like uninvited guests — too loud, too vivid, too much. Trying to "not think about it" only makes them louder. Containment gives your mind a safe boundary. Instead of battling the thoughts, you acknowledge them, then choose to store them somewhere secure until you're resourced enough to revisit them (ideally with therapeutic support). This isn't avoidance — it's wise pacing. By practicing containment, you send a message to your nervous system that you're in charge of when and how you engage. It builds trust with yourself, lowers overwhelm, and allows you to get through the present moment without drowning in unfinished business.

Visualize a container
Pick something sturdy — a jar, vault, chest, box, or even a digital safe.

Name the intrusion
Briefly identify the image, memory, or thought you want to contain. Write it in this jar here.

Place it inside
Imagine physically setting it in the container.

Seal it shut
Hear the latch click, see the lock turn, or feel the heaviness of the lid close.

Store it away
Place the container on a high shelf, deep cave, or secure room in your mind.

Return only with support
Remind yourself you can revisit it later with a therapist, journal, or trusted guide.

LESSONS IN INK

After hardship, the brain often circles around the why — why it happened, why you stayed, why you're still hurting. Meaning-making is a way to gently reclaim authorship. By naming what you survived and drawing out what it taught you about your own values and limits, you shift from being swallowed by the story to becoming the narrator of it. This process isn't about silver linings or forced positivity. It's about grounding your pain in context — saying, this mattered, this shaped me, and here's what I'm carrying forward. Closing with a boundary sets a line in the sand: you're not just reflecting on what happened, you're deciding how it changes the way you'll protect yourself in the future.

Headline: Write a short, bold line that sums up what you survived (as if it were on the front page of your personal newspaper).

Lessons: List 3–5 things it revealed about your needs, your limits, or your values.

Boundary: Write one clear, non-negotiable boundary you'll honor from now on.

ACTION

HOLDING HARD DATES

When difficult anniversaries come around—whether it's the day everything fell apart, a loss, or a traumatic turning point—the body remembers even when the mind tries not to. This can show up as anxiety, fatigue, irritability, or old grief bubbling back. Creating an intentional ritual allows you to meet those days with structure instead of being blindsided. By noting the date ahead of time, building in gentle scaffolding (like a support person, a nourishing activity, and less demand on yourself), you create a container for your nervous system. Closing the day with gratitude is not about being thankful for the pain itself, but for your endurance—that you lived through it, and you're still here. Ritual turns an overwhelming anniversary into a moment of honoring resilience.

Mark the Date
Note the anniversary on your calendar so it doesn't sneak up.

Plan Support
Choose one person you can reach out to if things feel heavy.

Nourish
Schedule at least one grounding or soothing activity (walk, bath, journaling, cozy meal).

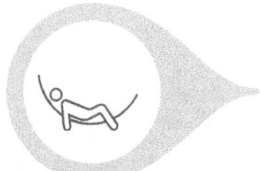
Lighten the Load
Keep your to-do list small that day.

Close with Gratitude
End the evening by writing or saying one thing you're grateful for in your survival.

ACTION

SAFETY IN SENSATION

After stress, trauma, or relational upheaval, our bodies often feel like a battleground—tense, guarded, or disconnected. Reclaiming the body is about coming back home to yourself. By practicing gentle, nurturing touch, you signal to your nervous system that it's safe to soften. This isn't indulgence; it's essential care. Daily attention to your physical self strengthens body awareness, lowers chronic tension, and reminds you that your body is a safe place, not just a vessel for pain. Over time, these small acts become proof: I can care for myself, and my body can be trusted again.

1. PICK A NURTURING TOUCH
Examples include rubbing lotion into your hands, sinking into a warm bath, wearing soft or comforting clothes, or even a gentle hand on your chest.

2. ENGAGE FULLY
Notice textures, warmth, weight, or scents — bring mindful awareness to the sensation.

3. BREATHE INTO THE TOUCH
Let each inhale gather calm, each exhale release tension.

4. PRACTICE DAILY
Even 2–5 minutes consistently signals safety and care.

5. NOTICE CHANGES
Check in with your body and note any softening, release, or increased comfort over time.

SECTION THIRTEEN

Living with the Longing – What If I Never Get the Family I Deserved?

There's a grief that doesn't get talked about enough — the ache for something you never had. The birthday where no one called. The holiday you spent alone. The ordinary, everyday warmth that others seem to take for granted. That ache doesn't always go away. Sometimes it softens. Sometimes it flares. But it's real.

You might find yourself asking: What if I never get that kind of love? What if I never have the family I needed? It's a question full of heartbreak. And also one that deserves tenderness, not dismissal.

This section isn't about pretending it doesn't hurt. It's about learning to live with the longing — not by shutting it down, but by giving it room to breathe without letting it run your life. It's about honoring the grief, even as you build a life that's deeply yours. One that holds space for both sadness and hope.

Making Sense Of It
The Empty Chair and the Open Table

There's a grief that never quite leaves — the quiet ache for family, for the ordinary warmth of birthdays, holidays, bedtime stories, or someone simply noticing you. For adults who grew up in foster care, this longing is complicated: part sorrow, part fantasy, part yearning for what should have been. And yet, the absence of that family doesn't mean your life is destined to be hollow. It means your heart has learned to carry multiple truths: love can be absent, yet you are capable of creating meaning and connection now.

Longing often arrives with questions: Will I ever experience this? Did I deserve it? These questions are not weakness; they are evidence of your relational heart. In foster care, you were denied consistent family presence. You may have internalized the absence as personal inadequacy or unworthiness. But longing is not proof of failure — it is proof of sensitivity, of capacity to care, of the human drive toward attachment. It is, paradoxically, both painful and vital.

This section is not about replacing or erasing that longing. It is about learning to live alongside it. When we ignore or suppress desire for family, grief often festers in the body — tight shoulders, shallow breath, stomach tension. By naming, honoring, and ritualizing the longing, you reduce its unconscious grip. You acknowledge that what you wanted — what you were denied — mattered. The body, mind, and heart all need that acknowledgment to release some of the tension carried for decades.

Making Sense Of It
The Empty Chair and the Open Table

There's also the reality that the family you long for may never appear in the way you imagined. That's devastating. And yet, holding onto the longing while creating chosen family, supportive friendships, and meaningful connections allows for repair. You do not have to replace what was lost to experience care, belonging, and love. The key is integration: recognizing the ache without letting it dictate your capacity for joy, intimacy, or agency.

Consider the metaphor of the empty chair at an open table. The chair is real: it represents what you lost, what you wanted, and what you never received. The table is also real: it represents your current life, relationships, and potential. By acknowledging the empty chair, you honor your grief. By opening the table to yourself — your chosen family, your community, your creative work — you expand the capacity to live fully even in the presence of longing. Both exist together, not as contradiction but as balance.

Your longing is also a guide. It reveals what you value, what matters, and what you yearn to offer others. It can inspire connection, generosity, and depth in adult relationships. It can motivate you to build structures of care that were missing in childhood. Paradoxically, embracing the ache teaches resilience, empathy, and wisdom that the "perfect" family might never have instilled.

What kind of family did I dream of having as a child?

Give yourself permission to name it — not as a fantasy, but as a reflection of your unmet needs.

What kind of family did I dream of having as a child?

Where does the longing live in my body? What happens when I let myself feel it?

Slow down. Tune in. Does the ache live in your chest, your gut, your throat? What might it need?

Where does the longing live in my body? What happens when I let myself feel it?

What do I feel when I see others have what I never got?

Envy, anger, numbness, hope — there's no wrong feeling here. Let it speak.

What do I feel when I see others have what I never got?

Have I ever told myself that it's weak to want love? Where did that message come from?

Challenge the old story. Wanting connection is not weakness. It's human.

> Have I ever told myself that it's weak to want love? Where did that message come from?

How can I honor the ache without letting it define me?

You are allowed to carry longing without it controlling your worth or direction.

How can I honor the ache without letting it define me?

What would it feel like to create chosen family, instead of waiting to be chosen?

This one might be vulnerable. But maybe it's time to explore a different kind of belonging.

What would it feel like to create chosen family, instead of waiting to be chosen?

SELF-COMPASSION BREAK

When stress, shame, or pain flare up, most of us go straight into self-criticism: Why can't I handle this better? What's wrong with me? That inner attack only tightens the spiral. Kristin Neff's Self-Compassion Break interrupts that cycle. It gives you three small handholds: recognition of your pain, the reminder you're not alone in it, and an active choice to soften instead of harden against yourself. With repetition, your nervous system learns that you don't have to white-knuckle through suffering or numb out — you can meet yourself with the same tenderness you'd extend to a friend. That shift doesn't erase the pain, but it changes the way it lands in your body. Over time, it builds resilience, because you're no longer abandoned in hard moments; you become your own safe ally.

Notice —
Pause and acknowledge: "This is hard. This hurts."

Kindness —
Place a hand on your chest or cheek and whisper: "May I be gentle with myself right now."

Common Humanity —
Say: "Others feel this too. I'm not the only one struggling."

POCKET MOOD LIFTERS

When life feels heavy, it's easy to forget what actually helps. In hard moments, the brain tends to focus on what's wrong, not what's available. An Antidote List is your preloaded reminder: ten small, proven things that shift your state even a little. These aren't grand fixes or instant cures — they're micro-adjustments that keep you from sliding deeper into the stuckness. Pairing an antidote before a hard task helps you face it with steadier energy; using one after provides recovery and closure so you don't carry the weight forward. Over time, this list becomes muscle memory — your nervous system learns, When I struggle, I have options. That's the opposite of hopelessness.

1 **List Ten** — Write down 10 things that reliably lift your mood (a song, a walk, fresh air, texting a safe friend, lighting a candle). Keep them small and doable.

....

....

....

....

....

....

....

2 **Use Before** — Pick one before facing a task you tend to dread. Let it soften resistance.

3 **Use After** — Choose another as a closing ritual. Let it tell your body, That part is done. I'm safe again.

SECTION FOURTEEN

A Life That's Fully Mine – Reclaiming Power, Choice, and Voice

If the system took something from you — safety, control, your voice — it makes sense if you've spent your life trying to get it back. Sometimes through silence. Sometimes through survival. Sometimes by trying not to need anything at all.

But now... maybe you're ready to do something else: reclaim. Not in a dramatic, perfect way. But slowly. Tenderly. On your own terms.
This section is about recognizing that no matter what's been done to you, you still get to define your future. You still get to choose how you live, love, rest, and rise. You still get to use your voice, even if it shakes. Especially if it shakes.

You were never just what happened to you. And even if the world never said it outright — you have always been worthy of authorship over your own life.

Making Sense Of It
The Pen in Your Hand

If foster care teaches anything, it's that much of your life — your home, your rules, your relationships — was dictated by others. Decisions about who you lived with, when you ate, where you slept, or even how you were allowed to feel were often made without your input. For many adults who grew up in the system, this can leave a lingering imprint: the sense that life happens to you rather than by you. It can leave a quiet fear of making choices, trusting your instincts, or speaking up — because survival once depended on compliance.

Reclaiming your life begins with a radical realization: you were never just what happened to you. You are not solely defined by the system, the homes, the trauma, or the people who failed to protect you. You are a sentient, capable adult with agency, wisdom, and a voice. The pen — symbolic or literal — is finally in your hand. Writing your story, setting your boundaries, making choices that honor your body, heart, and values — this is reclamation.

Choice, voice, and power are not abstract ideals; they are embodied practices. Every decision, from the small to the life-altering, is an act of authorship. What you eat, where you live, who you spend time with, how you manage conflict, how you care for yourself — all are ways to assert presence and reclaim authority over your life. Even when the world has been unpredictable or unsafe, these choices reaffirm that you exist as a sovereign being, not a passive participant in the chaos of the past.

Making Sense Of It
The Pen in Your Hand

This process is layered. Some days, you may feel shaky, unsure, or overwhelmed. Making decisions after a lifetime of limited agency can feel unfamiliar — even risky. That's okay. Reclaiming life is not about perfection or speed. It's about noticing that your preferences, opinions, and boundaries matter. It's about honoring what your body and heart say, even if the mind protests. With each choice, your nervous system practices safety and self-trust; with each boundary, it learns that your voice can be heard without consequence; with each act of self-assertion, it remembers that you exist for your own purposes, not for others' convenience.

Voice is central here. Many adults from foster care backgrounds carry the residue of silencing: being told to be "good," "quiet," or "grateful." Reclaiming voice is radical because it asserts that your words, thoughts, and feelings are valid. Speaking up — even softly, even shakily — reconnects your body and mind with the authority that was once denied. It tells your nervous system: I am here. I matter. I can influence my life.

Power is not about control over others. It's about sovereignty over yourself. It's the slow accumulation of consistent presence, self-advocacy, and intentional decision-making. It's the willingness to set limits, say no, and create conditions where your well-being is prioritized. By practicing power intentionally, you create a container in which your adult self can flourish — and your inner child, who once learned to survive unpredictability, can rest.

Where in my life do I still feel like I don't have a choice?

Start here. Be honest. Power can't return to you if you pretend it's already there.

Where in my life do I still feel like I don't have a choice?

What were the first moments I remember feeling silenced, dismissed, or ignored?

Track the roots. Give voice to what was lost, so you can reclaim it with clarity.

What were the first moments I remember feeling silenced, dismissed, or ignored?

What does power mean to me — not in theory, but in practice?

Does it look like setting boundaries? Laughing freely? Saying "I don't know"? Define it in your language.

What does power mean to me — not in theory, but in practice?

What parts of me learned to play small to stay safe? What do they need now?

Offer compassion, not criticism. Those parts were wise once. They just don't need to drive anymore.

What parts of me learned to play small to stay safe? What do they need now?

If I were fully free to choose my life — what would I say yes to? What would I say no to?

Let this be imaginative. Radical. Honest. This is your space.

If I were fully free to choose my life — what would I say yes to? What would I say no to?

What's one small act of self-leadership I could take this week, just for me?

It doesn't need to be huge. Even tiny actions plant seeds of self-trust.

What's one small act of self-leadership I could take this week, just for me?

EXTERNALIZE THE INNER CRITIC

The inner critic often masquerades as truth, when really it's a protective part gone overboard. By externalizing it — drawing it, collaging it, or writing it as a character — you create distance. Suddenly, it's not you failing; it's a scared or rigid part doing its job too harshly. Research in IFS and narrative therapy shows that putting dialogue on paper softens shame and restores self-leadership. Adding a Wise Friend voice gives you access to compassion and balance. The final boundary statement reminds the critic: its role is protection, not punishment. That's where healing starts.

Create the Critic — Draw, doodle, or collage how your inner critic might look. Don't worry about artistic skill.

Dialogue — Write a short back-and-forth:
You: "I hear you saying I'll fail."
Critic: "I don't want you to get hurt."
Wise Friend: "You can protect without tearing down."

Set a Boundary — End the dialogue with a firm line: "Your job is protection, not punishment. I'll take it from here."

MAPPING YOUR RESILIENCE

When life is painful, the spotlight lands on what's broken or lost. But every hard season you've lived through also carries evidence of your resilience. Mapping your past with a "strength lens" helps you reclaim those forgotten skills — endurance, creativity, boundary-setting, persistence, humor, or compassion. Trauma research shows that naming and revisiting these strengths rebuilds self-trust. Instead of seeing your past only as a string of wounds, you begin to recognize the ways you showed up for yourself. Circling three core strengths creates a personal toolkit you can consciously bring forward into your next chapter.

1 **Draw Your Timeline** —Mark a few "hard seasons" you've lived through on the timeline.

2 **Name Strengths** — Under each event, write one or two strengths you used to get through (e.g., courage, asking for help, persistence).

3 **Circle Three** — Look at the whole map. Circle three strengths that feel most alive, relevant, or needed for where you're headed now.

4 **Carry Them Forward** — Write them on a sticky note or card where you'll see them often — reminders that you've done hard things before, and you will again.

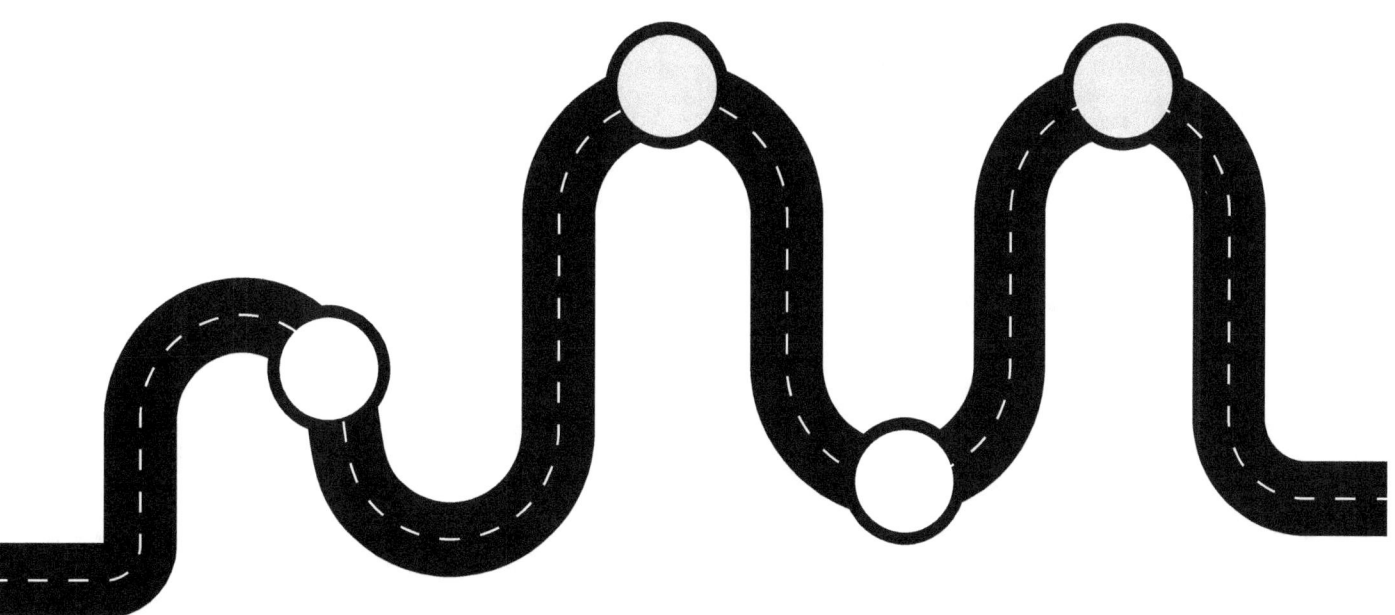

STONEWELL HEALING PRESS

ASSESSMENT

HOW FAR I'VE COME

You've done the work — now let's see where you're at. Take a moment to rate these statements again with honesty and self-compassion. Notice what's shifted, what still feels raw, and what that means for your next steps.

1-10

1. I feel like I belong in my own life — like I have a home inside myself.

2. I can face the pain of my foster care experiences without shrinking, hiding, or running away.

3. I can comfort and stand with the child I once was, even when they feel scared or abandoned.

4. II can make choices for myself without fear, guilt, or feeling undeserving.

5. I can experience love, connection, and trust without bracing for loss or betrayal.

6. I can speak my truth — even if my voice shakes, even if it feels risky.

7. I can hold the messy, complicated story of my past without feeling broken or "less than."

8. I feel I have the power to create a life that is truly mine — full of choice, meaning, and hope.

Mindset & Identity Shift Reflection

Healing changes the way you see yourself. You might notice you're less reactive in certain moments, more confident speaking up, or simply softer with yourself. This page is about spotting those shifts — the ones that show you're not the same person who started this journey.

In what ways do I see myself differently than when I started?

What beliefs about myself or others are shifting?

How has my sense of hope, strength, or trust evolved?

MOVING FORWARD

ACTION PLAN

This is your personalized roadmap for continuing growth beyond this workbook. Use this space to clarify which skills you'll keep practicing, how you'll notice early warning signs, and what concrete steps you'll take to support yourself. Remember, transformation happens one intentional step at a time.

Skills I will keep practicing regularly

Early warning signs or triggers I'll watch for:

When I notice these signs, here's what I will do:

MOVING FORWARD

ACTION PLAN

This is your personalized roadmap for continuing growth beyond this workbook. Use this space to clarify which skills you'll keep practicing, how you'll notice early warning signs, and what concrete steps you'll take to support yourself. Remember, transformation happens one intentional step at a time.

Ways I can check in with myself to monitor progress (daily, weekly, monthly):	
People or supports I will reach out to if I need encouragement or accountability:	
One commitment I'm making to myself right now:	

RESOURCE LIST

The resources listed here are shared for informational purposes only. While they provide valuable support and tools for mental health, I am not endorsing or guaranteeing the quality, effectiveness, or availability of their services. It's important to explore these options and verify the details directly on their websites to ensure they align with your personal needs.

National Alliance on Mental Illness

www.nami.org

Offers free mental health education, peer support, and a 24/7 helpline.

Insight Timer

www.insighttimer.com

A free meditation app with thousands of guided meditations, music, and talks on mental well-being

Parenting for Mental Health

www.parentingformentalhealth.com

Offers resources, training, and advice on how parents can support their child's mental health, including guides and printable resources

Crisis Text Line

www.crisistextline.org

Offers free, 24/7 text-based support for mental health crises

7 Cups

www.7cups.com

Offers free, anonymous online chat with trained volunteers, as well as paid therapy with licensed professionals.

The caseworkers are gone. The files are closed. Your name — scribbled on papers passed from hand to hand — now sits in a drawer somewhere, forgotten. But you're not. Even if you aged out, your pain didn't. Trauma doesn't expire. It lingers — shaping your thoughts, your reactions, your relationships. Sometimes it shows up as silence. Or hyper-independence. Or pride that says "I'm fine" when you're anything but.

You learned how to leave before you ever learned how to stay. How to pack your life into trash bags. How to sleep in beds that weren't yours. Homes that sometimes held you, and sometimes hurt you. Each move chipped away at something inside.

For some, the past is a blur locked in the back of the mind. For others, it still echoes every day. It touches your sense of safety, your relationships, your goals, your sense of worth.
And still, you survived. Not because the system worked — but because something inside you refused to quit. You grew through concrete. Stubborn. Unlikely. Still here.

This isn't about pretending it was fair. Or easy. It's about realizing that healing is still possible. That you get to choose differently now — how you show up for yourself, what you leave behind, and what kind of life you want next. This workbook can't fix what never should've been broken. But maybe, for a little while, it helped you feel seen.

We hope, wherever you go from here, you keep finding your way back to yourself — and toward the healing you deserve.

M. Tourangeau
Stonewell Healing Press

www.ingramcontent.com/pod-product-compliance
Lightning Source LLC
Chambersburg PA
CBHW060328240426
43665CB00048B/2843